Rainbow Goddess:
Celebrating Neurodiversity

Girl God Books

Edited by Kay Louise Aldred,
Pat Daly, Tamara Albanna
and Trista Hendren

Preface by Lucy H. Pearce

Cover Art by Kat Shaw

www.thegirlgod.com

Girl God Books

The Crone Initiation and Invitation*:* Women Speak on the Menopause Journey

The Crone Initiation and Invitation is an anthology of women's experiences of perimenopause and menopause, and the part Goddess plays in this journey. Crone's presence in the breakdowns and breakthroughs, the disintegration and rebuilding, is expressed through words and art. Meaning is reclaimed and the power of the Elder restored.

Mentorship with Goddess: Growing Sacred Womanhood

A Sacred Woman reclaims herself as Goddess – a unique strand, frequency and incarnation of her – essential for the completion and wholeness of the spectrum of the collective Feminine. Our bodies are the gateway to recalling this truth. Mentorship with Goddess is a workbook – a year-long curriculum and programme – a rite of passage – especially useful for the transition into autonomous adulthood – the process of individuation - and then also for the menopause journey.

Re-Membering with Goddess: Healing the Patriarchal Perpetuation of Trauma

Re-Membering with Goddess is an anthology of women's experiences of trauma—trauma as a result of patriarchy; trauma perpetuated by patriarchy; and how through personal healing of trauma the Goddess is re-membered, re-embodied and resurrected. As repeating loops of trauma restriction release—in the mind, body and nervous system— Goddess is re-embodied and rises... and the patriarchy falls.

Just as I Am: Hymns Affirming the Divine Female

What is a Hermnal? It's the collective sigh of our ancestral Grandmothers. It's a means of drawing us closer together as Sisters. It is a compilation of songs that affirm our Sacredness, apart from Man, and assures us that we are Sovereign Beings and Creatrixes, too. And it is our Love Gift of Gratitude to Mama.

In Defiance of Oppression – The Legacy of Boudicca

An anthology that encapsulates the Spirit of the defiant warrior in a modern apathetic age. No longer will the voices of our sisters go unheard, as the ancient Goddesses return to the battlements, calling to ignite the spark within each and every one of us—to defy oppression wherever we find it, and stand together in solidarity.

Warrior Queen: Answering the Call of The Morrigan

A powerful anthology about the Irish Celtic Goddess. Each contributor brings The Morrigan to life with unique stories that invite readers to partake and inspire them to pen their own. Included are essays, poems, stories, chants, rituals, and art from dozens of story-tellers and artists from around the world, illustrating and recounting the many ways this powerful Goddess of war, death, and prophecy has changed their lives.

Willendorf's Legacy: The Sacred Body

Travel through time and discover a world where the fullness of women was both admired and deified. Reclaim your beautiful Goddess body through the rich pages of this powerful collection of art, poetry and essays celebrating our divine inheritance as daughters of Willendorf.

Inanna's Ascent: Reclaiming Female Power

Inanna's Ascent examines how females can rise from the underworld and reclaim their power, sovereignly expressed through poetry, prose and visual art. All contributors are extraordinary women in their own right, who have been through some difficult life lessons—and are brave enough to share their stories.

The Girl God

A book for children young and old, celebrating the Divine Female by Trista Hendren. Magically illustrated by Elisabeth Slettnes with quotes from various faith traditions and feminist thinkers.

Complete list of Girl God publications at www.thegirlgod.com

"They sang the words in unison, yet somehow created a web of sounds with their voices. It was like hearing a piece of fabric woven with all the colors of a rainbow. I did not know that such beauty could be formed by the human mouth. I had never heard harmony before."
— Anita Diamant, *The Red Tent*

This anthology is dedicated to the rays which together unite and form Rainbow Goddess. This anthology is dedicated to every neurodivergent woman.

Table of Contents

Preface

Lucy H. Pearce

For most of my life I have tried my hardest not to be myself. I tried – and failed – to be what I saw as normal. Because I inhabited a world that kept telling me in small ways and large that there was something inherently wrong with me.

My core experience in this world was one of having my reality unheard or disbelieved. Again. And again. And again.

I became a good girl to stay safe.

I did everything I could to fix myself.

To make myself acceptable.

To make myself better.

This is the result of growing up an undiagnosed autistic person, daughter of an undiagnosed autistic person, and potentially the granddaughter of an undiagnosed autistic person in this world.

This is not just my story. But our story. The story of misunderstood creative, spiritually attuned, highly sensitive women: rainbow women.

My first book – *The Rainbow Way* – was written for that woman as a new mother. I came across the term Creative Rainbow Mother in the writing of Lynn V. Andrews and Leonie Dawson, and saw myself as clearly as in a mirror. I hungered to know more about her. And so, I wrote the book I wish I had been given upon entering motherhood, filled with the stories of so many creative mothers. My focus was mainly on the creative mother, because at that time I did not have the language to conceptualize what the rainbow part meant, beyond a rainbow of abilities, although I wrote at length in the book about highly sensitive women. I knew that this was an important piece of the puzzle, one that I had discovered via the work of Elaine M. Aron. But neurodivergence was a term that had yet to make it mainstream. Autism was still something that I – and my family doctor and children's school – thought only applied to little boys. I knew only that I loved rainbows, not that I was on the spectrum. None of us did. The majority of the creative rainbow mothers who shared our stories in that book have, in the intervening decade, discovered that first our children, and then ourselves, are in fact neurodivergent.

My generation of women have received our diagnoses or self-realisations after years of multiple burnouts and breakdowns, often after medication and treatment for mental health issues, which were not the cause of our struggles but a result of them. After a lifetime of being misunderstood and misunderstanding, we find ourselves here, now, in midlife, coming home to ourselves, whilst having to heal the decades of trauma and pain we have accumulated. We come with a lot of baggage. The next generation – our children – are being recognized earlier, receiving support, accommodations, and understanding as they grow into themselves. Their strengths and struggles are being met with greater awareness and understanding. My hope is that this will mean the first generation of neurodivergent folk starting out in life with a healthy degree of self-esteem.

Our children are emerging into the culture we have worked hard to create: a world where the rainbow – of gender and sexual orientations, skin colour, spirituality and neurology – are being embraced. Not everywhere. Not by everyone. But that is the way we are headed. It cannot come quickly enough. This is a time for all hands on deck. We face unprecedented times, times that call for thinking outside the box. We – neurodivergent folk – were made for these times. We have so much to offer.

Recognising our neurodivergence is not a way of cutting ourselves off from others, but a way into a more inclusive and truer

community. A like-minded community. At last, at last.
For many of us on the spectrum where expressing ourselves through speech can often be deeply challenging, we turn to the written word for self-expression. Books are our safe spaces of choice. They present us with accessible worlds, communities, and beings to explore, learn from and immerse ourselves in.

The collection of voices in this book includes many women whose paths have interwoven with mine over the last decade, both as real-life friends and creative collaborators. Birds of the rainbow feather most definitely flock together. Once we learn to show our colours, we find that we are naturally magnestised to those who see the world in a similar way, in whom we see ourselves, or a future version of ourselves writ large. When I read these women's words, I hear my own story shared in myriad voices. They are – we are, you are – creative rainbow women of the Rainbow Goddess: she of The Rainbow Way.

May you know yourself welcome here, met with love, whatever the colour of your particular neurology.

May you discover community and belonging here, within these pages, and in the world beyond it.

May we all be free to be more fully ourselves... and know that this is our most precious gift to the world.

May we find peace and acceptance and joy and healing.

May we dream a new world into being.

This I wish for you. Wherever you are.

The Power to Open
Lucy Pierce

Being a Neurodivergent Woman

Kay Louise Aldred

Many people, even my closest friends and family, have no idea that I am a neurodivergent woman.

Being autistic is still new to me as I was only recently diagnosed, in November this year.

I have done a great job at camouflaging, masking, and presenting as 'normal'. Neurodivergence was not something I had considered in relation to myself until I had children. This is ironic on many levels, most especially because I am a trained and experienced teacher and have held curriculum and pastoral leadership positions, in which I ensured that all students, from every demographic, including those who were neurodivergent, achieved their potential and felt safe, seen, and heard.

It was giving birth and rearing my own children which highlighted the 'differences' between me and my contemporaries, and significantly amplified the feelings I had been experiencing since childhood. Feelings of being 'atypical', 'odd' and a 'misfit'. Mother and baby groups, children's parties, and the PTA were mirrors which clearly reflected that I was not at all like 'most women'. They were also the situations where I began to recognise that my two sons bucked the communal childhood trends of behaviour, thinking and preference.

I did however socialise my three children well. Despite my personal discomfort around being in social settings and making small talk, I knew the importance of doing this. They thrived academically but when my sons transitioned to secondary school, I saw the hallmarks and signs of neurodivergence – predominantly sensory processing and autism. Their diagnoses were convoluted, unnecessarily complex in their procedure and stressful. I was told by professionals that I had 'taught them too well to be normal' and that 'they were coping' so didn't 'need a label'. They were both eventually diagnosed a few months before university, when it became completely apparent that the transition would only happen if they had support. The 'label' has been very helpful for them both in understanding and representing themselves.

Their diagnoses prompted me to assess my own lifelong challenges. My husband had been affectionately calling me his 'Aspie Wife' for a while before the penny dropped that I may be 'on the spectrum'. We operated as an autistic-friendly household – which helped everyone, including my apparently 'neurotypical' daughter (her ongoing journey of self-discovery is another story), long before I contemplated my own assessment. I looked on at both of my sons openly 'owning' their preferences and explaining their needs, and thought, 'I feel and have those additional needs too but am constantly pretending I don't'. I realised that the result of this pretence was suffering and an added burden.

That was four years ago. It is only now, aged 48 years, that I have got to the point of exhaustion and the resignation that I am not going to 'cure myself' or be miraculously transformed – and let me tell you I've tried all sorts of ways to do this, including, books, therapy, and spiritual practices.

Early last year I requested a GP referral for an adult autism assessment. Regardless of the outcome, I had begun to privately identify as neurodivergent, and noticed that acknowledging this went some way to explain the lifelong loneliness, social anxiety and chronic low mood I had experienced and offered a reason for the bullying and social rejection I had undergone – particularly as an adolescent.

On receiving the diagnosis last month, I wept. I felt numb, angry, grief stricken and elated simultaneously. Processing the magnitude of having an undiagnosed lifelong neurological and developmental 'disability' and coping with this alone, without reasonable adjustment, is going to take a long time. Autism is disabling in our society. And no, everyone is not a little bit neurodivergent or 'on the spectrum'. Knowing I am autistic has brought a new level of self-compassion and self-protection. I can't change myself or improve myself. Autistic people do not habituate – brain wiring does not change, and autism is not 'cured'. I'm curious as to who I am unmasked and what gifts that will uncover.

Some people who know me well, will be reading and learning this about me for the first time. I wonder if this 'coming out' publicly in the anthology will be liberating for the many women who continue to 'hide' their authentic self. The spirit of this book is the celebration of neurodiversity and so I'd like to channel that now and reclaim the Rainbow Goddess that I am by declaring that:

- I pretend to be interested in clothes. I'm not in the slightest bit interested. However, I'd happily wear the same thing every day – black cropped top, black pants, black vest top, black loose, jersey dungarees, black jumper, black socks with Ugg boots in winter and black sandals in summer. It's all about utility and minimal thought. I've got other things I'd rather think about.

- Tight clothes of any sort are a no. Why would I wear scratchy, restrictive clothing which squash up my intestines and womb and restrict breathing and digestion? Makes no sense.

- I intensely dislike small talk and prefer deep, philosophical, existential, and meaningful conversation.

- I find chit-chat exhausting – I don't understand it. It's a waste of energy.

- I'm not interested at all in hairstyles, makeup, or trends. I'm interested in the inner landscape of your life.

- I prefer my own company – listening to my inner guidance.

- I'm fearful of humans – the aggression, hostility, abusive dynamics, sarcasm, meanness, and inauthenticity.

- I trust very few people. Very few people are trustworthy and transparent.

- I am fiercely loyal – to those I trust and respect.

- I can't sequence – tasks, actions, to do lists. My brain is making patterns and connections about the meaning of life, justice, the universe. I may also have undiagnosed ADHD.

- I have zero executive functioning skills – packing to go on holiday puts me in a flat spin. Consequently, my home is a peaceful haven where I spend the most time.

- Synthetic lighting gives me a migraine – I prefer natural lighting and candles.

- Synthetic smells give me a migraine – I prefer nature smells and good quality essential oils.

- Perfume – NO!

- Organic, nature-based products only for my skin and in my home. Coconut, shea, and rosehip oil are winners. If I don't follow this, I have severe allergic reaction.

- If I go outside in sunlight without sunglasses, I get a migraine. My favourite seasons are late autumn and winter.

- I fatigue very easily. The best time of the day for me is 11am-4pm. I'm like a machine and can work those hours intensively back-to-back – productivity is high.

- Attending a large social gathering will take me days to recover from. I avoid groups of more than six. No offense. I prefer one-to-one.

- I have chronic motion sickness. I even get car sick driving myself. I'm a home bird. Did I tell you how delightful my home is?

- Many food smells and textures make me gag. Too many to mention. I was sick after being forced to eat beef mince at nursery.

- Plant-based, non-refined and non-processed foods suit my delicate digestion perfectly (and they're great for my overall health).

- Sugar, alcohol, and caffeine are not good for me in any way. I don't need any more stimulation!

- I am phobic of lifts, being in confined spaces and transport. I must know the exact route I'm taking and where the toilets are. I avoid motorways. I prefer country, scenic routes.

- Shopping centres give me a migraine, feelings of panic and nausea. The smells, music, lighting! I feel green just thinking about them. I like to shop local and support creatives and small businesses.

- I have dyscalculia. Numbers jump off the page. I used to hyperventilate in Maths class. On the flip side I am a word witch and genius.

- My coordination is appalling. My nickname as a child was 'Calamity Jane'. At least she was spirited – and probably Neurodiverse now that I think about it!

- I carried a dictionary around with me until the internet was available on my mobile phone. I may be a creative with words, that doesn't mean I can spell well.

- Giving birth and breastfeeding were traumatising. Not knowing when the pain was coming, when to push, why the baby was crying, how to latch on, how much sleep I would get. It was hard but I did it, three times.

- I don't like being hugged. Why lunge and grab someone without asking? I prefer a heartfelt 'hello'.

- My preference is always to be alone. No expectation or working out what is going on or how to respond.

- I can end up having a panic attack if neighbours are playing loud music. Why pollute the gentle, soothing sounds of nature and force me to listen to what you are listening to? Makes no sense.

- Being around people who are drinking alcohol triggers fear and panic. Their behaviour changes fry my nervous system.

- My 'special interests' are theology, spirituality, and embodiment. I'm endlessly fascinated by them.

- I don't really get you. I'll try and can read your patterns and energy and body, but I don't get you.

- I can't follow directions, recipes, or instructions. I prefer to freestyle and think outside of every box.

- My nervous system is highly sensitive and reactive – I have a lot of 'anxiety' and 'depression' in my system, which I manage every day. It's hard to stay alive.

- I feel like no one understands who I am. I don't really understand myself.

- I don't understand the world – even after being on earth for 48 years it still feels alien. Living is a quest.

- I am detail-oriented, persistent, and obsessive in relation to my passions. I'll research anything related to them to the greatest depth possible. As a result, I have a lot of knowledge to share (which I love doing and offer generously to those interested). I try not to 'info-dump' but sometimes it happens.

- I am socially phobic and chronically shy. I pretend I'm not to make you feel comfortable and in the hope I seem normal.

- I rarely express how I feel. I worry I will overwhelm you as I did my parents and family of origin.

- I hide how I feel. See above.

- I feel emotions in a big, embodied way. Somatic processing is challenging but essential and I can help others with this.

- I have the same getting up and going to bed routine every single day. The routine primes and anchors my day, reassures my nervous system, and makes things easier.

- I plan everything. Everything! So, I look like I'm coping, and you don't see my overwhelm.

- I see patterns everywhere – in words, shapes, nature, energy, food, and in you. It's beautiful.

Thank you for seeing me.

About This Book

Trista Hendren

Rainbow Goddess contains a variety of writing styles from people around the world. Various forms of English are included in this anthology, and we chose to keep spellings of the writers' place of origin to honor/honour everyone's unique voice.

It was the expressed intent of the editors to not police standards of citation, transliteration, and formatting. Contributors have determined which citation style, italicization policy and transliteration system to adopt in their pieces. The resulting diversity reflects the diversity of academic fields, genres and personal expressions represented by the authors.[1]

People often get caught up on whether we say *Goddess* or *Girl God*—or *Divine Female* vs. *Divine Feminine*. Personally, I try to just listen to what the speaker is trying to say. The fact remains that few of us were privileged with a woman-affirming education—and we all have a lot of time to make up for. Let's all be gentle with each other through that process.

If you find that a particular writing doesn't sit well with you, please feel free to use the Al-Anon suggestion: "Take what you like, leave the rest!" That said, if there aren't at least several pieces that challenge you, we have not done our job here.

We hope you find love, affirmation, and visibility in these pages.

---

[1] This paragraph is borrowed and adapted with love from *A Jihad for Justice: Honoring the Work and Life of Amina Wadud*. Edited by Kecia Ali, Juliane Hammer and Laury Silvers.

Rainbow Goddess

Kat Shaw

Hail and Welcome Rainbow Goddess, She of pure love.
Let your radiant beams of love flow over the world,
affirming that love has no structure, no boundaries,
no beginning and no end.
Fill me with the kind of unconditional love
that has no words, no form, no rules.
Love is… You. Love is… Me. We are one.

The Neurodivergent Goddess

Kat Shaw

To the Goddess who is impulsive, restless, and spontaneous.

To the Goddess who has an abundance of energy that cannot be controlled.

To the Goddess who is curious, asking never-ending questions, inventive, creative, fast-paced.

To the Goddess who has spent her whole life learning to compensate for her quirks.

To the Goddess who has learnt to suppress her natural instincts to conform.

To the Goddess who compulsively checks and organises to the extreme to avoid making mistakes.

To the Goddess who lives in fear of not living up to the expectations of others.

To the Goddess who berates herself every day for being different.

To the Goddess who never feels she does enough.

To the Goddess who tries desperately to keep her focus on conversations so as not to appear distracted or rude.

To the Goddess with social anxiety who tries desperately to learn how to fit in to society.

To the Goddess who constantly wonders what she will mess up next.

To the Goddess who dissociates when she becomes overwhelmed.

To the Goddess who cannot be still for a prolonged period.

To the Goddess who hyper-focuses and forgets there is a world outside the task at hand.

To the Goddess with the constantly racing mind.

To the Goddess who doesn't fit in.

To the goddess who is distraught at the realisation that there will never be enough time in the world to complete every idea in their head.

To the Goddess whose life is built upon a web of coping mechanisms.

To the Goddess who over-plans constantly to feel safe.

To the Goddess who feels like she is constantly letting people down.

To the Goddess who is burnt out trying to blend into what she believes she should be.

To the Goddess who has never found her place on the earth.

To the Goddess who feels so intensely that every emotion is all-consuming.

To the Goddess who feels numb because she has too many emotions that she cannot process.

To the Goddess who has shut down.

To the Goddess who doesn't feel safe with themselves.

To the Goddess who craves connection and company, but who struggles with social interaction.

To the Goddess who cries silently to herself.

To the Goddess who doesn't understand why she is rejected.

To the Goddess who lacks self-esteem and never feels enough. But also feels she is too much.

To the Goddess who overworks constantly because she doesn't feel worthy just being herself.

To the goddess who is called prolific, when really, she would love to stop but cannot.

To the Goddess who has to constantly justify her worth.

To the Goddess whose leg never stops tapping.

To the Goddess who is exhausted when she wakes up.

To the Goddess whose best friend is insomnia.

To the Goddess who cannot turn off that 1 line of a song going over and over and over and over.

To the Goddess who is compulsive.

To the Goddess who is obsessive.

To the Goddess who feels unsafe because the routine has changed at the last minute.

To the Goddess who always feels like she is on the outside.

To the Goddess who cannot focus.

To the Goddess who cannot regulate her emotional responses and then berates herself for acting up.

To the Goddess who is constantly tired.

To the Goddess who is always on red alert.

To the Goddess who beats herself up.

To the Goddess who does not stop. Ever.

To the Goddess who wants to be held.

To the Goddess who wants to be seen.

I see you.

I am you.

I love you.

And I hold you in my arms to breathe.

You are not alone.

Come back into your body because you are magnificent.

Exactly as you are.

Radiance

Lucy Pierce

Goddess Loves My Creative Neurodiversity

Tamara Albanna

The Goddess has many faces, or aspects, so why must we all be considered as neurotypical?

After a lifetime of trying to blend in, (more like disappear) I received an Autism diagnosis at the age of 41. This seems to be a common trend for women, especially. Due to the lack of access, and outdated beliefs still held about women and girls with Autism, it is often a fight to even get assessed. Then, of course, comes the question of access – assessments are expensive, and if you're lucky to be in a country where nationalized health care covers it, you're in for a year-long wait.

I was fortunate in that after spending a few years reading about Autism, and how differently it presents in women, I felt confident enough to seek out an assessment. It was some sort of bittersweet vindication; I felt that I wasn't meant to be like everyone else. The way I viewed the world, through a different lens, was perfectly acceptable and even "normal".

I remember my therapist lovingly saying to me, "I wish I could remove the word disorder, this is not an illness, you are differently ordered, you see the world in a different way, and we need that." Of course, my therapist was a woman – she didn't see a pathology, she saw potential.

I always knew I was different. It was beyond being the little shy girl growing up, it was something else entirely. My world, rather my inner world, was so incredibly rich, colorful, and diverse. It was a way to escape a traumatic situation and the confusion of not feeling like everyone else. I later learned that this inner world was "dissociation," and it probably is what kept me alive during the most trying times. I would "float" out of the classroom window, and into the clouds to meet all the fantastical beings, who were waiting there for me. On almost every report card, and at parent-teacher conferences, they would tell my parents that I never paid attention. I was always punished severely for this.

Navigating undiagnosed Autism, coupled with an abusive home life was a challenge, and something that I sometimes still feel the effects of as a woman in her 40s. But after abandoning patriarchal religion, I felt the warmth of the Goddess, often as the protective and loving mother I lacked and so desperately needed. When I came up against adversity due to my struggles, another aspect of the Goddess would present herself and I would feel strength. Most importantly, it was the compassionate aspect that I needed for myself. I often wonder if it was the Goddess leading me out of that window as a little girl, because it was the only time I felt safe.

The Goddess in all her aspects was a way to bring understanding to my own experience. Patriarchal tradition deliberately leaves out the feminine aspect, and this is so very harmful to women and girls. I would argue that it is even more so for the neurodiverse. Cold, hard, male-dominated science has tried hard to obliterate all the wise woman ways, and the traditions of our ancestors. Imagine the affect this has had on those who are not neurotypical.

I found acceptance in the Goddess tradition. It is by nature inclusive to us all and honors the differences among us rather than trying to "fix" us.

I often wonder how a matriarchal society would differently treat the precious neurodiverse children on the planet. Locked away, medicated, and shunned? Or brought into the light, embraced, and celebrated? I always imagine a beautiful world where all of us would be accepted simply for being who we are. Where the neurodivergent are looked at as a benefit to society, not a burden. There would be no need for children to float out of classroom windows, they would already be at home. We are not all meant to be the same. Just look at all the Goddesses around the world.

Bad

Kay Crowder

They said
if I followed the rules
I would be good.
And being good was the highest goal
as a girl.

Because to be bad
was to be rejected,
dropped,
abandoned,
left behind,
love withdrawn.
Therefore, it made sense
I should *always* follow the rules.
If I was good
I would be loved, forever.

But sometimes
I broke the rules
by accident
and the world didn't end.

I called myself bad anyway,
worthless,
unworthy of love
and I suffered for it.
I did it myself.

I drew the unworthiness and
the shame inside
into a little hard nut
in my heart
and there it lay
while I watched those
who would abandon me
be indifferent.

I abandoned myself
I punished myself
I said, "I am soooo bad."
Feel bad, Self.
Feel shame,
feel unworthy,
loath thyself
you rulebreaker, you.

"You are a blight on society
you don't fit the box
you breached the cage
you bent the bars –
the rules were the bars!
You are wrong,
we are right,
you don't belong
you must go."

And so, I said,
"Wait, what if I am ok
if I don't fit the box?"

Can being myself
be a Radical Act of Defiance?

Is being myself,
being BAD
a *bad* thing?

Maybe the biggest tragedy
was rejecting myself
once I found out
the rules were only stories
they told me
that had been told to them
and people before them
in order to keep us
small
tidy
obedient
caged
downtrodden
out of the way
because to be Big
Messy
Disobedient
Upstarts
Blocking the way
Taking up space
was to throw a wrench
in the order that kept
them rich
powerful
whole
strong
safe?

What if as
Messy
Loud
Smelly
Outrageous

Women
Children
the Radical Act of Defiance
is loving ourselves
as we ARE
before we are conditioned
to fit into the boxes
they created for us?

"You are ONLY
worthy of our label 'Normal'
if you fit into our box
that we defined
and forced others
to bend and form
their big round bodies
to fit into these boxes
THEN you can live
in our world

and you will be safe!"

That is the rule.
You fit into this box.
The promise is safety.

But, world,
you lied to me before with
your rules
and your boxes.
You said,
if you do this,
then you will be happy.
but you lied.

I was not safe
or loved
or whole
even after I did that
EXACTLY.

You left me then.
Said, "It's your fault...
YOU must have done
it wrong, because
my rules are always right
the boxes are safe."

And I shrank back
and abandoned myself
to the bottom of a shoe
for 11 years.
I betrayed myself
And believed your lies
that I was small,
deficient,
unworthy,
and had to hide away
In order not to cause
more fuss.

But the fuss found me
anyway!

So where are your
promises now
as I waver
on the precipice
of a gigantic
Big
MESS

where behind me
are your rules
and your world
and your empty promises
your boxes
and cages
and down below
is a void
of unknowing
but possible
freedom
to be myself
exactly as I am,

as only I can ever be?

Broken Glass, Spiderwebs and Rainbows

Deborah A. Meyerriecks

Never fitting in.
Never feeling good enough.
Trying to do everything on my own.

No one sees the hours or days or months or years it takes to start something or finish something. Never being able to ask for help because I haven't figured out what I need next and when I do figure it out in a sudden flash of either understanding or inspiration, if I don't handle it right away... it's lost.

No one understanding why I can't just say what I need help with so they can help. They take it upon themselves to decide I didn't actually need help; I just like to procrastinate. After all, whatever it was is done and in their opinion, perfect.

Parents praise the easy A's though high school while getting everything they asked for to be done, done. Never actually seeing any homework getting done. Proud praises became confirmation of meeting expectations. Honor Roll Society, again, naturally, of course Deborah got Honor Roll. The tedium of successful repetition became an expectation that bred boredom.

Not understanding why I was floundering in college. Realizing I never learned how to study and in high school, you are told exactly what they will test you on. In college, it's conceptual with an attention to detail you provide yourself.

Learning how and where to get the necessary information – and how to process and regurgitate it – breeds Impostor Syndrome. Whether it was in small study groups or metaphysical subjects or the NYC*EMS Academy. As people would show up to my study table the hour or three before exams and I would share what notes I created for myself and my tips and tricks to remember what to do and in what order... Order of operations; same for mathematics, chemistry, and patient assessment. Trust me on this.

I never felt good enough to be the teacher, but I could share what I was studying and learned thus far. This became impromptu pop-up classes on everything from Calculus to Trauma Assessment to Basic Astrology and How to Be a Witch.

People would call me a teacher. I wouldn't. I was sharing what I read, what I learned. My view of looking at the information, analyzing the data, and sharing the resulting information. If I can do this, anyone can do this. Right? Imposter Syndrome grows.

Learning to be cautious never to take credit. Always citing sources and references. Completely missing the point of what a teacher is and does. Year after year, month after month, day after day, I was astounded that anyone would come to me to learn anything. If I knew it, everyone would already know it. If I can look it up and learn about it, I'm probably the last to know about it.

They think I'm humble.

I'm really scared.

What if, just like the transition from high school to college, I fall on my face, get overwhelmed, and fail. I know I can just withdraw from classes I'm due to teach just like I withdrew from my 2nd semester of college. Walk away and disappear. No one would miss me. Who even thinks about me when I'm not there? Who loves me when I'm not useful? What if I screw up while acting as a guardian and guide while the person who entrusted me dives deep and starts to do the work of learning what they need for their own productive shadow care? What if their trust in me is misplaced?

How much was from the trauma I was subjected to and how much was actually my brain processing things differently but being told I was never going to succeed and, "if you worked for me, I'd fire you." (Yep, that was my mother). And so often never being allowed to begin – unless you not only could see the end, but all the steps and stages in between.

My daughter is an absolute Rainbow Warrior Goddess. I'd like to believe that doing my own shadow work and shadow care enabled my amazing Dynamic Duo to become the creative, intelligent, insightful, and considerate adults they are today. That I've given them their space to develop their own communication style as well as helped them to learn common communication skills to help communicate with "normal people."

My daughter has ADHD. Her willingness to talk with her friends about what she was feeling and experiencing, especially when feeling overwhelmed, led to shared experiences and language to use to best explain and represent what is helping and what is making things harder for her. Day to day, class to class. Her doctor listened. Suggestions were made. Medication offered as part-time help but not touted as a cure or a solution. Reassurance that what she lives with is a gift as well as a curse.

Gift and curse.

The openness and willingness to let my Dynamic Duo tell me anything without interjecting or correcting or "helping" unless asked. It led to her sharing her diagnosis with me. But not until after she shared what she does and how she does it with interjections from both of us that I do the same thing. She let me know that although a doctor would have to diagnose, I most likely have high-functioning ADHD with burnout.

Oh My Goddess! I believed she was right.

Now, I have more to read and research and digest and either incorporate into my living routine or discard as not relevant or helpful for me. It matters. It helps. I don't have writer's block; I need to catch the right understanding of how to get to what I need to write about and how I want to express it.

It's not that I'm a slob or lazy. Executive Dysfunction. It's why I can find an unconscious patient and figure out what they need and where to take them in split seconds but I can almost never answer the question "what do you want?"

It's probably why I count everything. Quite literally everything. And even the things I don't realize I am counting, I am keeping cadence. My son and daughter are my Dynamic Duo. They are my great detectives. They are the ones who told me I always stir my cup of tea 13 times. "Of course, you do, you're a witch and it's probably a spell you do, right?" Um, maybe? Unconsciously? In my head as I stir I always hear a 1-2-3-4, 1-2-3-4, 1-2-3-4-5 and it just doesn't taste the same if I can't do it for myself.

My daughter is diagnosed and has had guidance to learn ways to help her thrive even better than before. She has set up her current home to create exactly the sanctuary she needs it to be. She can communicate with her partner what she needs while also hearing what they dialogued and try to make space for both of them. She opened dialog with potential roommates and facilitated them to be able to express what they want and what they need when it comes to sharing an apartment together while working and going to school.

My son enjoys his solitude while bonding with friends through the joy of the internet. It's actually how he met his current partner. Truth be told, it's how I met my current partner of 4½ years. They are planning their new home around what both need to be their best selves. For themselves and for each other. There is a learning curve. They have learned the communication skills they need which include stating when one of them is feeling overwhelmed and just needs to hit the pause button on whatever they were discussing. They survived house hunting during the pandemic. I think they have solid ground to continue to grow together.

They are both incredible peer counselors and often I ask where they heard or learned what they said to someone because it was so perfect. I'd like to write it down and cite it for future use with my own 'clients' and peers. Me. They remind me it was stuff they overheard from my helping others talk through stuff often enough that it comes easily to them. All they did was speak from their own experience and thoughts as they instinctively personalized whatever they said for the person they said it to.

I am learning. It's a process. Through the sometimes planned yet often spontaneous shadow work, I'm learning who I am, who I'm becoming, and who I've always been. The more I understand what neurodivergency may or may not involve, the more I understand why I have acted and reacted in certain ways.

I'm also learning that all the reasons I previously expressed for not being comfortable calling myself a teacher are all exactly what makes me a teacher. I can refrain from calling myself an expert or being fluent in any particular topic. One doesn't need a masters or doctorate to be a good teacher. I will always acknowledge my limited scope of education and cite my sources. I will always take ownership and responsibility when expressing my own opinion or anything I've never seen cited elsewhere.

I have discussed Goddess Whispers elsewhere. What I mean is that at times when I suddenly feel like I can talk with authority about something – then realize, I don't have the education or accreditation – I have no reason to know what I suddenly know. I perceive the information as divine inspiration. Typically, I can feel whether I can trust the source, even if I'm not able to cite it to anyone's satisfaction.

So often I feel like my thoughts are racing by so fast that if I don't document them immediately, I've lost them permanently. Other times there is absolutely nothing cognitively happening, and I can hear the lights. I can hear the wind. I can hear what people tell me doesn't make any sound. But when the thoughts are racing, I hear nothing else if I catch that wave and for as long as I'm willing and able to ride it, nothing else exists. It's how I'm writing all of this for you right now.

There are days where I am so tired, I can't even talk. Then a flash of inspiration, triggered by something unexpected, and I quite literally need to either drop everything else I was doing, or physically make myself get up and go to my laptop or it's lost. If you surf, you know what it means to miss the wave. You can't get it back. There will always be another wave. You don't know when a surf-able one will come. Even if you are watching and waiting you never know if you will be ready for it, but you do know it won't be the same no matter how good it may be. Also, floating, drifting, watching, and waiting are boring.

Boring isn't bad. It's comfortable. It's calm. It's safe. It's also usually nonproductive. The fastest way not to finish something that needs to be done, is to perceive it as boring. And when you start to feel like you need to do something. ANYTHING. Boring is a death sentence. The body at rest will stay at rest while complaining about having nothing to do. YET the pile of dishes in the sink and papers all over in need of organizing or shredding, and the pile of laundry builds. It builds by the day, the week, the month. If it isn't urgent, it doesn't get done.

Ritual provides a comforting routine. Morning cacao or tea with my Goddess. A particular candle holder getting a new tealight or votive candle on my family altar. The requisite 2 minutes of sunshine in my face (longer is OK but skipping it is not) to fulfill my promise to myself, my family, and deity to start some self-care daily.

Start daily. Continuing is hard. Starting is easier. Picking a small daily task and doing it brings a sense of accomplishment. What did I do yesterday? I washed a cup. You know, I have a dishwasher. It wasn't full and the sink was empty. But with no energy and having a high pain day and my brain's emotional impermanence which hits me with "if he isn't initiating communication and he isn't telling me he loves me, then he's bored with me and that's sad for me." And that hits even harder than Imposter Syndrome and feelings of inadequacy. Maybe it's because they go hand-in-hand.

Three normal breaths. Call to my Goddess. See where the breath feels stagnant. Which cauldron is blocked from refilling? Which is blocked from emptying and thus spilling over and making me feel a sloshy mess inside?

The Three Cauldrons are Warmth (the Coire Goiriath), Vocation (the Coire Ernmae), and Knowledge (the Coire Sois). There is a fifteenth century poetic tract (found within an ancient Irish legal manuscript) that describes the body as containing Three Cauldrons rather than Nine Duíle. This metaphysical treatise's composition is credited to Amergin, the Milesian Ollamh and to Nede Mac Adne, Chief Ollamh for Conchobhar Mac Nessa. The relative positions of these cauldrons within each person was thought to determine the overall health of a person as well as the state of their mind and psyche.

It describes how joy and sorrow affect the first two cauldrons causing them to pour out, empty, overflow or become dry. Why is this even significant? Because in my journey to understand myself better I decided to discover the name of the goddess who spoke to me. I traced family heritage for clues. Eventually I found Her when I wasn't looking but She was ready for me to know Her by name. My mother's mother's mother was born in Ireland. I'm American from NYC with family roots somewhere south of Shannon.

I've studied the Hindu Chakra system and have learned enough to understand there is so much more I have to learn. But I do have a working understanding. The Celtic Cauldrons are not an Irish Chakra system. I can clearly see how both systems operate independently yet function in symbiosis within all of us.

I have learned through fostering a deeper relationship with my Goddess is that She demands authenticity, honesty, and respect. And She expects you to give it to yourself. In order to be honest and authentic, I needed to accept and gain an understanding of who I actually am for me. As that understanding becomes clearer, as I peel off and throw away the performance expectations that were put on me like so many layers of tinted film on a window, I began to see myself for who I truly am. As with a clear window, it's easy to see the scratches, chips, and cracks. Certain ones we can fill in and seal, others we may buff smooth and polish. Some we might decide to tap a little and create lovely patterns that enhance our own uniqueness. No one looks at an artfully etched glass and thinks it's ruined. They think it's a masterpiece that took time, patience, and loving talent to craft.

Slowly I am turning individual cracks into a spiderweb of intricate beauty which will eventually reveal the mandala of my life.

And when I hold it up to let the sun shine though, I'll cast rainbows over all around me.

And yes, I just made myself cry. While I have never thought this before, it rings absolutely true. My curse, my gift. My magick, my spirituality, my Goddess, my family, my life. Crystal Rainbows gifted by Goddess but we can only see them when we are willing to open our eyes to the light we shine from within.

News Headline 2030
The Future is Neurodiverse

Kay Louise Aldred

Society Steadfastly Stabilised and Unified Thanks to the Neurodiverse Rainbow Task Team

The chaos and division of the last decade is finally subsiding as steadfast stabilisation and unity is being restored in society thanks to implementation of the vision for change and wellness transformation offered by the Neurodiverse Rainbow Task Team over the past year.

The vision – 'Creative Calm' – is proving to be beneficial to all aspects of health for neurodiverse and neurotypical people alike. The task team holistically analysed the needs of individuals and organisations from all demographics of society and found neurodiverse-friendly ways of living had the most positive impact on all participants. Participants and organisations have now adopted neurodiverse living and working strategies, which prioritise regular rest breaks, working according to personal energy rhythms, plant-based nutrition, maintaining states of low conflict and stress, clear communication based on expressing individual needs and preferences and cultivating creative passions.

Personal wellbeing and organisational productivity have soared. Interpersonal tensions and disputes have been minimised. The whole pilot scheme was a resounding success. Life and job satisfaction increased exponentially and there were affirming outcomes for workplace and family harmony and cohesion. A nationwide and possibly global initiative of change and vision application are now underway.

So, what will this mean for you? The core vision includes the following suggestions:

1. Transparent, non-abuse, mutually respectful dialogue integral to every workplace
2. Zero tolerance of aggression in any form
3. Unique talents sought out and celebrated
4. Creativity and critical thinking paramount
5. Overhaul of educational practices – mixed economy teaching and learning – in person and on-line lessons, smaller class sizes and bespoke curriculum pathways
6. Strip and fluorescent lighting is now illegal in work and public spaces
7. Biophilic design mandatory in all public spaces
8. No loud music in public places without a licence
9. Mandatory quiet areas and acoustics in all public, work and education spaces
10. Flexible working hours
11. Adjustment of working practices according to the seasons of the year, especially weather and daylight changes
12. Hiring and work practices adapted to individual strengths – a wide range of presentation methods mandatory including art, visual, audio, technological

ND Prayer

Trinity Shea Thomas

I am not flawed.
I am custom designed
To deliver
Embodied solutions
For our world.

Help me bridge
So we can map
Our new way forward.

April 2022

Listen

Arna Baartz

Truthtellers

Jen Wallace

We are the sensitives
The seers
The truth tellers
The pattern weavers
The medicine folk, the healers
The soul retrievers;
The edge dwellers
The storytellers
The holders of the myths.
We sense the dangers
We see the signs
We sound the warnings
We feel the tides
We carry the songlines
And the dances of dawn
In our hearts.

We are the gentle folk
The innovators
The creators
The vision makers
The risk takers
The game changers.
With passion
And focus
We notice,
And with
Purpose
And calling
We achieve
The amazing.

We are
The descendants
The sisters
The brothers
Fathers, mothers
We are
The children
Of the ancestors
We are the kin
Of the birds
The beasts
The plants
And trees,
The bees.

We are
The land
The water
Walking
And talking
And we
Are beginning
To remember
The old ways
So that
The new ways
We forge
Are those
Of hope
And belonging
And connection
So deep
That our
Souls
Stop longing
And we
Are at peace.

Terminal Misunderstandings

Jen Wallace

It feels like
We are listening
To each other
Underwater.

I don't
Understand
The subtext
The context
The expressions
And intonations.

All
I hear
Are
The Words.

And I have
No idea
How to wrap
My Words
In a package
That
Proclaims
Their
Sincerity.

Yet, I can feel
Our souls
Reach for each other,
Fingertip to fingertip,
Even as you
Walk away.
And I will grieve that part
Of you
That always wanted to stay.

Ayida-Weddo

Kat Shaw

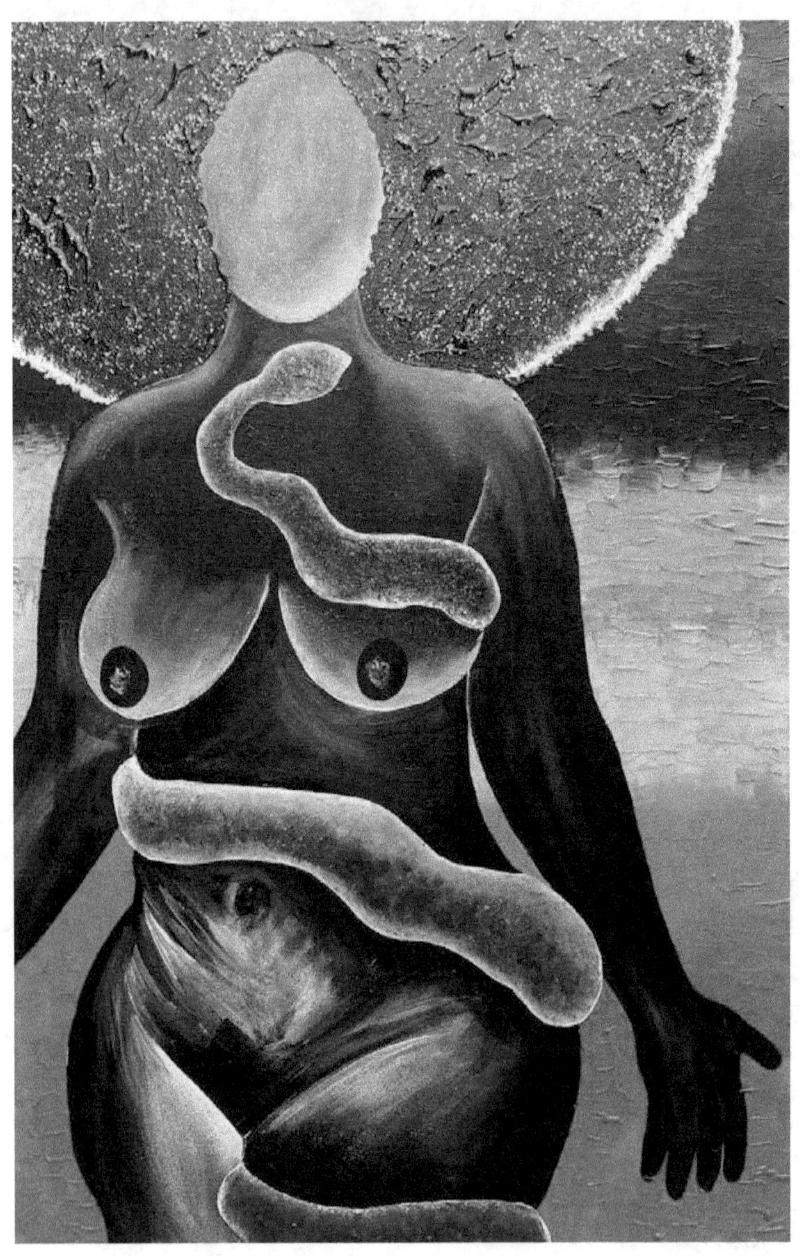

I am Ayida-Weddo
Haitian Rainbow Serpent Goddess.
I bring a message of peace and strength to humanity.
To come together as one for unity.
Holding up the heavens, I will rain fertility and blessings upon you.
I bring balance to male and female.
I bring balance to the Earth.
I am the shedding of the old.
I can hold the universe.

Being Diagnosed with ADHD at 46-Years-Old

Kat Shaw

I have spent the entirety of my life trying to learn the rules.

I have tried consistently to fit into a society that has always felt a bit out of my reach.

I have tried to navigate what does not come naturally to me.

And I have learned to wear a mask brilliantly.

I have built an identity that the world sees.

One that fits in to society's perception of "acceptable".

I have learnt to speak at a relatively normal volume, even though I want to shout.

I have learnt to not butt into conversations every 2.7 seconds.

I have learnt to live with a song or phrase replaying in my head 7 million times a minute, consistently.

I have learnt to remain focused on a conversation even when I want to look out of the window.

I have learnt to live with the fact that some days I do all the things, and some days I am too overwhelmed to do any of the things.

I have learnt to force myself to do things that don't interest me to keep on top of life (paying bills, accounts, etc).

I have learnt to live with about 739 thoughts in my head at once.

I have learnt to speak words that I want to sing.

I have learnt to remember every special occasion and get birthday cards delivered on time, even though I often forget and then beat myself up for weeks.

I have learnt not to get overwhelmed with my environment and get rid of all my belongings.

I have learnt not to overthink every small thing, yet still do this constantly.

I have learnt that I hyperfocus on some things and forget I have a life outside of my body.

I have learnt that I binge eat to light up the reward centres in my brain.

I have learnt that I overspend for the same reason.

I have learnt to stop calling myself stupid and thinking I am a failure for not being able to carry out menial things.

I have learnt that generalised anxiety disorder and ADHD is a tricky mix to live with, yet am very good at hiding this.

I have learnt to always try and remain on guard for information needed as I forget everything approximately 3.6 seconds after I am told it.

I have learnt that I crave dopamine and will hunt it down everywhere.

I have learnt that rather than using my "survival mode" to keep me safe for a phase of my life, I actually live in it.

I have learnt that I send 8 texts in a row instead of 1 combined message, which annoys people. Yet I cannot stop.

I have learnt that I will eat the same food for 6 weeks every day and then never touch it again in my life. And this is not balanced or healthy. Yet, it happens.

I have learnt to read and pretend I am focusing on a book, yet that actually reading it is almost impossible – however much I want to.

I have learnt to live in a body whose brain never switches off – ever.

I have learnt to carry spares because I lose everything.

I have learnt to stop tapping and jiggling even though I want to move all the time.

I have learnt to live with imposter syndrome as my best friend.

I have learnt that I have to google every single character in a film and often miss the storyline.

I have learnt that I am extremely obsessive. And extremely compulsive. And impulsive.

I have learnt that I feel things much deeper than the average person, yet try to hide my extreme reactions.

I have learnt that colours are brighter to me.

I have learnt that I cannot hear what you are saying to me if I can feel that I am wearing my clothes.

I have learnt that in order to find the way when driving I need to turn the music down.

I have learnt to live when my eyes dart in 285 directions every second.

I have learnt that I struggle with time blindness. Therefore, I am either 2 hours early or 2 hours late.

I have learnt to live knowing my brain is different than others.

I have learnt that I have never felt worthy as I have never shown my true self.

I have learnt that a structure of coping mechanisms are needed to function in my day-to-day life.

I have learnt that I cannot switch tasks quickly if I don't want to, which results in distress if I need to.

I have learnt that I will not remember your name, so have come up with rhymes to try and remember. They generally just end up buzzing around my head and I still forget.

I have learned not to throw away food packaging immediately otherwise I have to get it out of the bin because I have forgotten what the instructions to cook are.

I have learnt that I must force myself to go out, otherwise I will be a hermit. Even though I make plans, I often regret doing that as I have to be "normal".

I have learnt that I wash clothes, forget to hang them out, wash them again and forget to hang them out again. Repeat.

I have learnt to set timers on my phone throughout the day to remind me to do things.

I have learnt that I can only hear the TV if I have subtitles on.

I have learnt that I am distracted by anything, so my inner dialogue has to remind me to remain focused.

I have learnt that I have felt permanently guilty for no reason for as long as I can remember, so try to say kind things to myself.

I have learnt to tread on eggshells as I constantly think I am going to do the wrong thing.

I have learnt to think before I speak because if I feel out of control, I get angry.

I have learnt not to scream if someone moves something of mine.

I have learnt that in life, I am all or nothing. And that's the way it is.

I have learnt not to overtly and unnecessarily over share.

I have learnt to try and just talk about 1 topic at a time.

I have learnt that my music does not have to be on at full volume.

I have learnt to restrict my online time so as not to lose 5 hours researching pointless information.

I have learnt that if a text message or email gives me instructions that I don't understand and that have to be actioned, I ignore it.

I have learnt to be OK with the fact that I miss all the deadlines.

I have learnt that if I have 1 task I don't want to do, it stops me doing everything else.

I have learnt to dissociate to survive menial tasks or situations.

I have learnt not to cry at least 4 times an hour.

I have learnt to live feeling like I don't belong anywhere.

I have learnt to remind myself that my best is good enough. But I do not truly believe this.

I have learnt that I need to make space and time to mourn for all the years I was unable to maintain friendships.

I have learnt to live always feeling like I am playing catch up.

I have learnt that I am not broken, however much I feel like I am.

I have learnt that it's OK to cry for the little me that never felt they were good enough and didn't understand why.

I have learnt to block out stimulus in order to concentrate.

I have learnt that if I try and hold a thought in my head, it'll disappear, so I carry a notebook at all times.

I have learnt to stop fidgeting.

I have learnt to screenshot messages on my phone and then check them at the end of the day so I remember to answer.

I have learnt to simply "like" something instead of letting it consume me.

I have learnt to be busy to take my mind off reality.

I have learnt that my worth depends on how hard I work to prove myself, so I never stop.

I have learnt to tell myself it's ok to relax sometimes. Yet still cannot.

I have learnt to live with constant exhaustion.

I have learnt to rush everything in case I forget what I am doing.

I have learnt that burnout is real and yet I still push through it.

I have learnt to try and control my constant craving for new experiences.

I have learnt to learn from the reactions and facial expressions of others.

I have learnt to suppress my true needs.

I have learnt to mentally script and rehearse conversations before socialising.

I have learnt to behave in socially acceptable ways. Even though that is not the "real" me.

I have learnt to try and pretend to be interested in topics that other people are talking about.

I have learnt to live in a constant state of overwhelm.

I have learnt to be over organised to avoid the anxiety of missing something.

I have learnt not to zone out.

I have learnt that my brain tells me constantly that I am flawed.

I have learnt to hide my struggles from others.

I have learnt to be a people pleaser.

I have learnt that I am a perfectionist, so I just work harder to try and make things perfect.

I have learnt to install a key safe outside my house as I forget my key almost every day.

I have learnt to live with constant, chronic overwhelm.

I have learnt that I never fully relax.

I have learnt that my rapid and intense mood swings come from feeling triggered and that I am not just an arsehole.

I have learnt that my risk-taking doesn't make me simply a careless person.

I have learnt that my migraines often begin if I feel burnout, excessively mask, or try to control my stimming.

I have learned that I have to work extra, extra hard to fit in.

I have learnt to live with mental exhaustion.

I have learnt to adapt to the thought that everything I do is not quite right.

I have learnt to live feeling constantly in trouble.

I have learnt to become more reclusive as this is when I can un-mask and be me.

I have learnt that nobody sees or knows the real me.

I have learnt that if too many people from different places come together, I have to maintain the personality I've created for each one at the same time.

I have learnt to live with constant fear of rejection.

I have learnt to cut and run immediately if the slightest thing goes wrong.

I have also learnt that sometimes the things I think are going wrong are totally made up in my head.

I have learnt that my perfectionism makes it hard for me to set personal boundaries and know when to stop working, so I continue to overwork.

I have learnt to set unrealistic expectations for myself.

I have learnt to stare at a computer screen for 5 minutes and having absolutely no idea what is on it. The same goes for written instructions.

I have learnt that I wake up exhausted.

I have learnt that I need people's full attention to feel heard – yet struggle to give my full attention to anything.

I have learnt that I don't chew my food.

I have learnt to live with feeling like a constant annoyance to everyone.

I have learnt to take a breath in between sentences, even when I don't need to.

I have learnt that the desperate need to know every single minute detail of a conversation is not really the done thing, so try to suppress my need to ask, yet cannot listen to the rest of the story without knowing.

I have learnt to live with random energy shutdowns when things get too much.

I have learnt to walk when I want to run or skip.

I have learnt to force myself to meet new people face to face after online interactions, even though the fear of being found out to be a "fraud" is often crippling.

I have learnt to read the same paragraph 7 times before I even catch a glimpse of what I am reading.

I have learnt to stop myself putting my success down to just luck instead of hard work and ability.

I have learnt not to fixate on the things I did not do well.

I have learnt that comparing myself to others is not good for my mental health.

I have learnt to live in a structure which keeps me safe as I know what is coming next.

I have learnt also that I feel imprisoned within a structure. So, this Is a constant contradiction.

I have learnt to live in a house full of post-it-note reminders.

I have learnt to mask my behaviour to look like a neurotypical person.

I have learnt that my worth comes from fitting in.

I have learnt that an adult diagnosis of ADHD is different from a child diagnosis, as you mourn the years you've beaten yourself up because you didn't know any different.

I have learnt that society classes me as having a "disorder". This wording is not ok.

I have learnt that I have built a totally false outer representation of who I am.

I have learnt to sit with this sadness deep within my soul.

I am learning that I am OK just the way I am.

And every day I am learning to unlearn what I have learnt to learn who I really and truly am.

I'll let you know when I find her.

Got Myself Some Flippers Now

Jen Wallace

I don't regret
The years I spent
Doggy paddling
On the surface
Using all my energy
To stay afloat,
Focusing
On not drowning.

But it was when I went under
And then opened
My eyes
That I
Discovered
I can dive.

I can dive deep
And there are
Wonders down here
That
Are beyond description
And I'd love you to come too
But
You got to take
That dive yourself
And
I need
To let you know
That I'm
Not a surface swimmer
Anymore.

Ajna

Kat Shaw

Fly with me to the higher realms of perception.
Bridging your consciousness to deeper intuition.
Raising your vibration.
Rising always.
I will help you to see beyond the veil.
To reality.

From Weird to Wyrrd: My Journey to Wholeness as a NeuroDivergent Woman

Arlene Bailey

I've always known I wasn't part of the herd. Always known I think and see differently. I made up words and said words differently. That's just how my brain worked, and I loved the amazing visuals and word weavings that, even as a child, came to me.

Fitting in though... Ooy! As a child and young adult, I tried to fit in. I tried to mirror my behavior and dress after those seen as the most normal and, ironically, the most popular with parents and teachers and ministers. I realize now that was how enculturation worked. Teach a child to be just like the adults in her life (who were already enculturated to behave in the herd) and you've got another member of the "you must be like everyone else club". You know, the herd! Otherwise, you were seen as having something wrong with you.

College was the same. A bunch of rich kids from large cities and then little ol' me on grants and from a small town in another state. I was once again different, not accepted and I knew it and it hurt. Though I made good grades, I struggled in school (college too) because I didn't understand like others, didn't see things like others and that made me different. Even in my family, it was a problem in that my younger brother and sister, like my dad, had photographic memories and remembered everything. That made it easy for them to regurgitate what they were taught. Not so for me as I just could not see things the way they did, or the way others did.

I learned though to play their game and hide my genius for that's how I learned to see myself compared to the Cookie Cutter mold of what masqueraded as normal. But I was an Outsider. I still am actually – though most outside my inner circle would never know

because I've learned to hide it so well. No one would ever know –
no one ever sees who I was/am beyond the Plain Jane child,
teenager, young woman, and now elderly white woman that most
see. That is, unless I allowed them to see beyond their filters.
Even then most would say oh you're not like that. You're so
normal. No. I Am Not.

If only they would really look, really see me, but they do not.

My dream world – both waking and sleeping saved me as did the
stories I told myself and the pictures I saw in my mind's eye. I
could go anywhere in my mind and had the most amazing
experiences that in no way could be articulated, but for some
reason I could write about them.

So, I wrote and wrote and wrote and lived in my own little world
where I was safe and not judged and could be the non-conformist
that in my heart and mind I knew I was.

Sadly, though, I didn't feel safe in their world, so I continued to
conform and dress like the others, trying to look and act like
everyone else. But those like me recognized me. We were kin, not
of this world and not part of the cookie-cutter herd.

I felt trapped though and longed to be free to be whomever and
whatever I was for I'd never placed a label on myself except to say
and know I wasn't like all the others. That hurt – a lot – for many
times all it would take was one look at me and I was dismissed as
substandard, different, weird. It wasn't until I learned that
"weird" came from "wyrrd" and that made me special. That's
when things became to change.

Oh, I didn't really change outwardly – well, yeah, I guess I did in
that I no longer cared what anyone else thought. I did and said
what I wanted, went where I wanted and even began to dress and
look differently.

My family definitely did not understand or approve nor did most of my friends. So, I got new friends who became my family. People more like me who willingly accepted my quirkiness and eccentricity and very, very different way of seeing and knowing.

I'm a Crone now and I celebrate all my wyrrdness in its most extreme form. I write and paint things most will not. Write about things and paint images the "normal" crowd – the herd – doesn't like nor understand. But now when they look at me and say you're "weird", my eyes light up and I see "WYRRD" and I say "Thank you, it's my best quality"!

I really abhor labels, but when I read about the term Neurodivergent, it felt like home. I do see things differently, think differently – actually can think circles around most people... well most neurotypical people. Even when I try to explain something they don't get it. But... people like me do.

We... I... may not be the norm – you know the herd mentality – but, Oh My Goddess, Thank you, Thank You, Thank You for creating this Daughter from a different mold, using different clay and forging her in purple flames so as to create a gem so rare and exquisitely unique as to be able to walk her own path.

More and more I am finding freedom in being who I truly am and I LOVE it when people say... "you are so strange, so weird, so out of the box of normal, etc., etc." My reply has become: *Thank you for actually seeing me for I adore every wyrrd cell and thought in this body that once again walks the Earth in this time as a woman out on the edge of what is seen as normal!*

Arlene Bailey, ©2022

I Never had an Escape Plan

Jen Wallace

Has difficulty with transitions
Isn't just
The 6-year-old
Melting down
Because he has to leave his Lego
And go
On a family trip.

It is the 17-year-old still at the party
At 3 AM,
Long after
The 'good kids'
Have gone home.
Still drinking
To hide
The confusion
And disorientation
Because
She cannot
Even start
To imagine
The steps she would need
To take
To leave.

I Come Here to be Me

Jen Wallace

We are old hands at this,
This windy shore and I.
These crashing waves
Have heard
Me scream
And dance,
Sing,
And cry my own ocean.

They are my steady witnesses.
Whatever I hurl is welcomed
And I am never too much
For the sea
And the sky.

Talking Through Autism:

Auto-Ethnographic Reflections on Participating

in UK Autism Support Groups

Kim Crowder

In early 2020, following diagnosis, it mattered a lot to be able to use just three letters, ASD, to encapsulate the tensions between the positive and problematic aspects of myself. But I was confused and uncertain. How could I better make sense of my autism? I needed to talk, so when the NHS based county autism service invited me to join a support programme, I instantly signed up.

Weekly two-hour sessions, held in a community hall, were attended by around twenty people from a wide variety of social, educational and employment backgrounds. Ages ranged from twenties to sixties. Activities included presentations, discussions, and facilitatory exercises, each focused on exploration of specific aspects of autism. Group rules stipulated no interruption while others spoke, no dismissal of others' opinions, no swearing. Based on my own recollections, notes and journalling the following section revisits not only what we talked about when we talked about autism, but also how it felt to talk through our experiences of autism – and to allow autism to talk through us[2].

Empathetic encounters

We always begin by writing down a worry, putting it into the Worry Bowl, then selecting someone else's worry to read aloud, a process that de-personalises our worries. We spend time talking about worrying about the car breaking down, being late, what to

---

[2] To protect the identity and privacy of group members, names of individuals, autism support agencies and locations are excluded from this account.

say, being misunderstood, fear of unknowns. We worry about the room, the people, discussion topics. Some of us are worried by crowds, airports, trains, others by the intolerable sensory pressures of the working environment's phones, lights, temperature, and noise.

The facilitators say that our worries will be consistent, lifelong – but here, our worries about talking about worries will diminish. We persist in talking about the difficulties we have with talking in group situations. In pairs, we discuss reactions, feelings following diagnosis. Some mention shock, others relief. Some describe relatives' inability to understand the condition. Some express guilt at having passed autism onto children and grandchildren.

Meltdowns and bewildering arrays of traits are outed. There are some who stay silent, unable to get a word in edgewise because one of their traits is difficulty with joining conversations.

The facilitators talk about coping strategies: giving ourselves time, rehearsing challenging events, writing scripts, not attempting too much. They introduce mindfulness. We try it before being encouraged to verbalise our feelings about a non-verbal experience.

There is relief at not having to explain that we are autistic, because here we're all autistic. We can lower the mask. Some disclose that they have allowed themselves to act "more autistically" since diagnosis. We trade examples of the huge effort that "acting normally" entails. We examine others' disbelief of our autism, those who say, "You don't look autistic." We formulate replies: "So what does autistic look like then?" or "Shall I start head-banging?"

Each week the all-female facilitators introduce a new topic – what autism is/isn't, sensory issues, crisis points, masking, disclosing, communicating, compulsions, special interests. Hand-outs are distributed to prompt brainstorming, but we go off-topic often, relapsing into talking about worries: How to cope when bad things happen, handling work-load, meeting deadlines, wondering where to sit, offending someone, making mistakes. In the conversational loop that repeatedly returns us to our worries, we are and aren't talking about what we're meant to be talking about. The facilitators introduce 'wellbeing', defining it as "a state of physical and mental contentment, calmness of mind".

Wellbeing involves optimism, feeling strong, experiencing good self-esteem, and not worrying. Some of us conclude that we rarely experience wellbeing.

We're shown a diagram of a pyramid marked with labels: At the apex is 'self actualisation'. Someone asks bluntly "What's that then?" The answer is that it involves "identity needs, fulfilment of ability, ambition, personal achievement, reaching potential". Unconvinced, the questioner calls those things "a dream" and "not possible". The facilitators ask what happens when our wellbeing falters. We say we crash, burn-out, lose control, meltdown. We upset others, get illnesses, self-isolate, consider self-harming, refuse food, experience anger, lack of motivation, hopelessness, depression. We feel lost, suicidal. When asked how we cope with such feelings, we list computer gaming, avoiding people, avoiding situations, self-isolating, wearing noise-cancelling headphones, taking photographs, spending time with pets. We learn about 'social energy' and 'social accounting' via a diagram illustrating the large energy tanks of extroverts: These tanks drain slower than those of introverts who have small, fast-draining tanks. Asked what we do to re-fill our tanks, we say we walk, crochet, sew, listen to music, weight-lift, swim, draw, read. Our solitary pursuits equip us with the energy to be social.

Being physically close and interacting for two hours is demanding. We sometimes lapse into wordlessness, yet the unsaid is communicated via the stimming that accompanies our talk and our silences. Intently we knit, doodle, hair-twiddle, fingernail-pick, foot-jiggle. We spin, pop, and click custom-made stim toys. Like this, we stay in touch with our bodies while connecting with our thoughts: Through certain sensory inputs we generate the energy needed to focus on the topics, the thoughts, the words we must find to talk our way into and through the outing of autism.

Pressures and aftereffects

What effect did these sessions have on me? My overriding memories are of a deluge of information from both facilitators and participants; urgency; intensely charged atmosphere; accounts of personal distress; empathetic reaction. Sessions often raised more questions than answers, but lack of any structure for out-of-session contact between us prevented deeper one-to-one exploration of issues raised, therefore I had the contradictory sense of being attached to a group but also being alone with what I learned. Although better informed, I was no better connected with autistic others as knowledge-making did not translate into networking.

Often the facilitators appeared stressed, struggling to cover the planned content as so many questions took us back around the worry loop. They fell victim to their own rule regarding allowing others to speak, not butting in, so within a live situation where raw emotions surfaced, timetabling often went awry. This mention of the facilitators' predicament is not a criticism, but instead highlights the extent of their workload, the demands placed upon them by growing adult diagnosis numbers alongside shrinking public health funding. The group was the only NHS sponsored one serving an entire county, therefore long waiting lists and large group sizes resulted.

The power of presence

My background reading didn't prepare me for the effects of encountering autism in the flesh. Often, peoples' intense narration of worries and traits amounted to far more than spoken description: It felt as if the entity of autism itself was being

summoned by us, amongst us. During discussion, the condition
that brought us together, the thing that we not only resisted but
also valued became an almost tangible presence, both with us and
of us as we brought it into the open. Although painful at times,
this externalisation of something routinely hidden and masked
was positive. The impact of seeing and hearing many of my own
feelings and experiences mirrored in others' accounts was
revelatory, reassuring. I saw them in me, me in them, all of us in
autism, autism in all of us – all of this present within the room.

In describing autism's 'presence', I do not impute any negative
characterisation to the condition. What I saw bore no
resemblance to sinister portrayals presenting autism as a
problematic, invasive impairment in need of eradicative 'cure'. By
contrast, the group context revealed how participants
performatively produced autism's myriad qualities – both negative
and positive – through speaking them, feeling them, being them
and doing them. Each person brought their own ASD life-story,
their own unique constellation of ASD traits and effects, their own
understandings of ASD's constraints and affordances. Although
people spoke as individuals, what emerged was a richly nuanced
compendium of ASD's elements and effects, made through the
collective endeavour of piecing together myriad fragments that
transcended a mere listing of 'symptoms'. Such detailed
knowledge seemed inherently valuable, something to work with
rather than against. But there were questions: How might that
presence and knowledge be captured? What benefits might result
from sharing it ?

Motivations: moving on

My use of the pronouns, 'we' and 'us', is not based on any idea of
speaking *for* other group members, but instead indicates that I
spoke *with,* alongside them. The experience of talking through
autism has taken time to process. Then, my position was as a
receptive novice participant accessing an expert-led psychology-
based service. Now, I occupy a different position, more confidently

my own ASD self. Equipped with knowledge learned in group contexts, I've become more free-thinking, more proactive, better able to manage my ASD. I've realised that ASD itself – as well as medical and cultural understandings of it – are not static, but constantly alternating between life-stages and generations.

This account is offered from the perspectives of first-hand experience, empathy, and advocacy. One of its motivations is my concern with the problem of how to capture, share and optimise group-generated knowledges of ASD, but two years on, and despite my experience of academic writing, I'm left unsure about what I can and can't do with my group-acquired knowledges, what uses are and aren't permissible, what destinations are amenable to such knowledge. Auto-ethnographically inflected accounts of adult autism are as yet scarce, and any relating to adult female autism even scarcer. A barrier to addressing this knowledge gap attaches to confidentiality since rigid adherence to formal medical protocols or group-specific rules regarding privacy, risks the stifling dissipation and diminution of knowledges generated by group-based autism support practices. Who owns this knowledge? Who controls its purposing? Who grants permissions? Undoubtedly certain ethical and protective protocols are vital, yet my experience suggests that in their current absolutist form, prohibitions on dissemination can risk a polarisation of knowledge destinations and usage: Some knowledges may be relegated to the 'blogosphere' while others, acquired via the funded research culture, may be formally appropriated as academic 'property' and situated beyond public access. The current absence of a middle ground between social media and academia – and lack of clarity regarding who can say what where – matters in relation to autistic peoples' self-knowledge, autonomy, needs and, crucially, their often under-acknowledged capabilities and aspirations.

Considered first-hand accounts of lived experience deriving from group settings could potentially advance understandings of the condition itself, especially regarding the newer categories of female / late diagnosed adult autism, and crucially, could also contribute valuably to the long-overdue construction and recognition of autistic-led culture and community – the 'dream' of self-actualisation, or wellbeing.

One of the Covid pandemic's social effects has been the explosion of virtual meeting platforms. Since relocating to a different part of the UK, I have attended numerous online autism support events. Their vibrance and democratic nature has demonstrated how the whole landscape of autism support and interaction is undergoing radical and positive transformation, but the sense persists that existing protocols are neither matching the current pace of change, nor fitting the needs and wishes of increasingly vocal and highly articulate autistic people.

I don't consider myself an activist, but in moving between 'we' and 'I', subjective and objective, what is now and what might be, and in discussing the problematics of 'ownership' and the purposing and positioning of group-generated knowledge – I point towards a new discursive space, a new writing territory which I hope others will also explore and develop: What is necessary now is autistic-led writing and commentary that responds to and moves with, the autism and the diversifying autistic voices of our times.

Chasing the Moon
Or, Finding Your Strength and Voice

Kerry Purdy

All that I'm going to say is, I'm so happy that the idea for this compilation was conceived. I have been through so, so, much, and have so, so many things to say... so much that much of this essay will likely seem like a jumble, myself pouring myself out, and so forth. But bear with me!

What is "neurodiversity" and how does it tie into spirituality? Glad you asked. Neurodiversity ranges from any sort of neurological wiring deemed divergent from the so-called "norm" – Autism, ADHD, and tons of other things. But, however, what is the "norm?" If you ask me, what our society deems as "normal" really isn't that bright, intelligent to be honest.

But, however, how does spirituality, goddess culture, paganism, etc. tie into this? I'll make a confession: I'm not really as into goddess culture per se, as I am Celtic and Norse practices. But there are many, many ways that many of these deities and practices tie into neurodiversity!

First of all, let's go a bit into neurodiverse females. Neurodiverse females, if you ask me, are *especially* in need of powerful, divine feminine energy – and I believe that many, if you ask me, will find out that they had it inside them all along... an incredibly strong, powerful, fierce side underneath what many see, at least initially, as a soft, weak-willed exterior.

There is, indeed, a very fierce, fiery, take no shit side to autistic females – and you'll see it after a very short period of time. Morrigan has indeed always been with me. But right now I want to give another example of a deity that may not be the first one that many think of at all... Hati Fenrirsdottir!

For years, I honored the Tuatha De Danann, the gods and goddesses of Ireland. My great-grandparents immigrated to the United States as teens from Westmeath (*my great-grandmother was born not too far from the "cave" said to be sacred to Morrigan!*) and Galway, respectively. And for many, many, years, I clung to Irish everything... I brought up my Irish heritage to everyone. I made sure that people were aware of it. Why? Because I thought that if people associated me with that country, they'd think that I could fight back easily and would leave me alone because of that.

And Morrigan, and the rest of the Tuatha De Danann are, and always will be, very near and dear to me. They will be my first and foremost. However, in the last few years, another pantheon has been coming to me... the Norse! And not just the "light" ones such as Odin, Thor, Freya, etc. The Rokkr as well... the Jotun. The "dark" deities... dark, but not "evil." And this is where my interesting encounter with a wolf-goddess named Hati comes in.

For those outside the realm of Norse practices, Hati, as well as her sister Skoll, may not be familiar. But most are aware of their father, Fenrir, the enormous wolf demon who is prophesied to usher in Ragnarök (do I believe that we are on the verge of said event? Yes, but that's a story for another time). Fenrir is, like most of the Rokkr, a very dark god... but not exactly evil. He is destruction incarnate – what we honestly need to usher in a new and better world. His children are Hati, who chases the moon, and Skoll, who chases the sun.

It was a Monday (day of the Moon – keep that in mind) last fall when Hati came to me. For years my throat chakra had been badly blocked (by my elementary school trauma, no doubt – as I said, I was a very strong-willed, assertive child before that – I wasn't easy for anyone!) Finally after many, many years, a Reiki practitioner was able to unblock it for me – and that fiery, sassy girl, now a strong powerful woman, came straight back! But I'm getting ahead of myself.

So, I got the guidance of Hati Fenrirsdottir, telling me to go to a YouTube video that helps with the throat chakra. As I meditated to said video, more came up in my mind – it was, again Monday, not only the day of Hati and Mani (the moon-god that she pursues) but the day of Mercury as well – the planet that facilitates communication. As I ruminated more on that thought, the words came to me, *You deserve to have your throat chakra open. You deserve to speak your truth.* And I do.

My blocked throat chakra was, as I said, almost entirely due in part to abuse by a sick, sick, teacher in first grade. But I have spent my whole life feeling ignored, not being listened to, my opinions being thrown aside. That and my first-grade trauma? (followed by plenty of other cruel and abusive situations?) No wonder my throat chakra was badly blocked!

Most neurodiverse women and girls do not originally start out timid and submissive, as so many come across. But as I said, from a very young age, they start being alienated, shamed, pushed aside, and forced to "fit in." That, not autism, is what blocks the throat chakra. And the fact that girls, regardless of how their brains function, are all too often taught to be "nice?" Really amping it up. (*One thing that does need to be kept in mind is that many individuals with autism were born to late-in-life parents. Many autistic women and girls were brought up the way that girls were brought up in the 1940's and the 1950's. Be meek and sweet in all circumstances. Everyone is innately good. Everyone has your best interests at heart. And many end up sadly finding out the hard way that that is indeed not how our world works.*)

Neurodiversity is misunderstood. Hati and Skoll – hell, the Rokkr, hell, alternative religions, period, are misunderstood. But really, there's nothing wrong with being "outside of the box." It has been said that, in the case of autism, some believe that said neurotype may have originated millennia ago in Europe to give an advantage in hunting and tracking. If that is indeed the truth, look at how essential autism would have been to our early hunter-gatherer societies. Autism may have ensured that our early ancestors didn't starve. And all these years later, a world removed from primitive hunting, the essential need for autism could be coming back... in the cyber age. My Homeland Security professor, who was extremely well-versed, high ranking Air Force, and very likely having a good deal of autism himself (and that's a compliment to him) said that the next massive terrorist attack will not be planes flying into buildings. It's going to be a major cyber-attack... and it will bring the world to its knees. Many of the soldiers that I serve with in the Ohio Military Reserve would tell you the same thing... and I can see where they're coming from. Our world has every right to be terrified of a massive cyber-attack... and it may have to be autistic brains that end up saving the world if (when?) that does happen. In my mind, the gods – the Tuatha De Danann, the Aesir, the Vanir, the Rokkr, etc. don't make mistakes. I personally find it eerie (in a good way) that, just as our world becomes dependent on everything cyber (the Covid pandemic moved it even further along)... a whole huge wave of people are coming (autism cases are increasing...) that have the exact mindset for this type of world... as well as the protection and stabilization of said world. It's just like Hati and Skoll's father; he's seen by many as a vicious demonic monster that will end up being the downfall of us all – and has no redeeming qualities. But others don't see that. Our world is outdated – and he will be essential to sweep out what no longer serves us – and make way for the new. This is why I'm glad that the Rokkr/Jotuns came to me – they teach us balance – nothing is purely good, nothing is purely evil.

As I said, Irish will always be first and foremost. But the Norse indeed did invade Ireland and intermarry with the native Gaels. My upper body strength, cold tolerance, blood type A, light blue eyes... yep, you can see it in me! I'm not excusing the terror that they brought to the shores of Ireland... (they didn't just *intermarry* with the Irish, let's just say...) but I'm grateful that they introduced me to their deities. In many ways, there are similarities between Hati, Skoll, and Morrigan.

Hati Fenrirsdottir isn't widely known outside of the Norse pantheon – but she's become a staple presence in my spiritual life, as well as her sister Skoll, her father Fenrir, and of course Uncle Jormungandr (the World Serpent.) Hati pursues the moon – and in her pursuit of the moon, she also symbolizes those of us who chase our shadow side... our true self. I am a strong-willed, assertive person – and I am entitled to speak my truth... for myself, and for others... and maybe in time teach others to find their voices as well.

Everyone deserves to have a voice.

I picture Hati and Skoll at times as large wolf-creatures, but often as humanoid women with wolf ears and tails – Hati with long dark brown hair and piercing blue eyes, Skoll with long light red hair and red eyes... both dressed in the armor of a Norse shieldmaiden / berserker. (Too bad I can't draw – I would totally draw them!)

For the last couple of years, I've been having vivid dreams... and many involve the Rokkr Gang... Hati, Skoll, Fenrir, and Jormungandr. (Others make an appearance as well, namely Odin, angels, and even the Virgin Mary.) I would like to share a couple that pertain to this essay (copied and pasted from my blog):

I walked through doors into some sort of building – like a hospital, knowing what I was going to find there. The place was quiet and empty, and then after I had taken a few steps through the doors, Fenrir appeared in the hallway. He instantly grew to a monstrous size, and Hati, Skoll, and Jormungandr all appeared beside him. I heard in my mind, be not afraid, this must happen, this world is outdated, it must end to make room for the new – and I instantly saw Fenrir swallow the moon, which had turned to blood.

Instantly before waking up, I heard myself saying, "And so it begins."

I was sitting in a grassy, sunlit meadow and the feeling was very peaceful. I saw none other than Hati and Skoll, the wargs that chase the moon and sun, standing in the meadow. They also looked very peaceful, and Skoll even let me come up to her and pet her like a horse. Then clouds rolled in, and the sky became black as night... but through the clouds I saw the moon turning orange. My thought before I woke up was, "It is fine, it must happen."

I have plushies of Hati and Skoll, by the way. Both by Squishable! 😊

Woven

Jen Wallace

There are threads that
Run through them all:
The lost years
The soul drying, dying, party years,
The shame years
Playing the
Wrong game
Years.
The finding years,
The healing years,
The anxiety and panic years,
The year long years,
The day long years
The moment that's ten years.
My given years.

I stand here
Now
Woven
With knotty threads
Of resilience
And hope
And the strength of
My mother
In my ear
All those years
Reminding me
Of my worth.
And my grandmothers
In my other
Ear

Mumbling spells
For my protection
Bound
With the threads of
Rosary beads
And daisy chains.

Divergent Super Power

Kathy Barenskie

I'm tired of hearing,
"S/he must be a little Autistic; she is so rude."
"We are all on the Spectrum somewhere."
And this being said to describe the awkward, unsociable side of someone's personality.

There is an Autistic Spectrum, however only people with Autism experience it. In actual fact, there are days without a sensory issue or confusion. This is when I am high functioning on the spectrum.

Don't minimise my experience of being me, by throwing out a casual comment. You are not on the spectrum. You're blurting out an awkward truth that reflects being less thoughtful for that day. If I happen to do that, it's because I genuinely missed the social norms.

Being Autistic does not have to equate to all the social faux pas, it brings many gifts. Although I will speak generically, as we share many traits, I can only speak for myself here, as every one of us are uniquely different.

Us Autistic people experience life through our bodies. Our sensory abilities are amazing. We have a highly compassionate empathy, (although there is much literature and misconceptions regarding our cognitive empathy facilities). We easily can access the other non-ordinary realities. It's easy for me to see and talk with my guides and other Spiritual Beings.

I can feel vibration dind can actually feel the presence of what are known as Angels and higher beings. Often Elementals take form and sit with me a while.

As a child I was always on the outside looking into other people's realities, while being locked inside my own special world.

My dreams would take me on adventures where dreamtime blended with reality, until I didn't know what was what. I would see tall, glimmery white, beautiful people in the trees and sunshine and waters and grasses. The winds would speak to me in breezes. And the nighttime brought dark figures in the shadows and talking animals.

I learned to 'feel' people as a means of working out who was good and not so good. Also, to take on others' 'sickness' and hold it for a while in my body, to give them a break. This is my energetic, inward experience of being Autistic.

Although my childhood memories are shrouded in a veil of confusion and sadness. I never quite could figure out what was going on. I was more than vulnerable and experienced abuses no child ought to go through.

More than any of the abuses, it's the confusion that I hold onto now. All the other stuff I have worked on, and they no longer create a block in my body, my life. On into adult life I have continued seeking relationships, religions, belief systems, looking for that connection with other people.

The poem I wrote (on the following page) is about the seeking to find the 'authentic being' in the people I meet. Sometimes it's hard to find the spark behind the mask.

My world is full of colours, and I want you to know that being Autistic is a superpower.

Rainbow Goddess Self-Portrait

Kathy Barenskie

Alien Brain

Kathy Barenskie

"Autistic

Wired differently.
Disabled thinking leads to a dysfunctional life.
Or so they say.

Alien brain full of colours and sounds.
5D living in a 3D world.
Energies jumping out at me.
I look and look trying to find some semblance of their humanity?
They catch me staring.

My body leaks pain.
It sits like a poison on my tongue.
It strikes out like a snake.
Because to bite is another way to communicate.
To bite them open,
so they leak their authenticity.

I am hyper-empathic so it hurts to be present to their noises,
their dullness.
Always cracked,
a bit weird.
That crack is where the hurt gets in.
My container is cracked.

That crack is where the Love gets out.
The golden stuff,
you know,
love?
that rises up the spine.

That foundation on which relationships are built.

They couldn't handle all of me,
I'm too much.
Their sameness and dullness would fade them out to distinction.
So I shift my shape to fit their shadow.
Drip feeding myself in small pieces, so they can tolerate my spicy
flavours.

My eyes look and look,
trying to discern,
who are they really?
All the time,
figuring out,
It's exhausting!
Eventually I adapt,
so that they are more comfortable,
and can be present to my bright colours.

But my container is cracked.
I don't understand myself,
So how can I possibly understand them?
Alien brain,
more human being,
than all their human doing.
Brain full of colours in a flat grey world.

An Open heart.
An Alien brain.
A Rainbow mind.
Autistic."

Rainbow Goddess Rapture

Barbara O'Meara

You Drew Your Stars Differently Right From The Start

Back in the day there was no label or name, but what there most definitely was a deep sense of shame. Off to school as a very young child, already a sinner but still meek and mild. "Your writing is wrong, your capitals all slumped". Full fists on the back as you were unexpectedly thumped. "Can't do your sums, hold out your hand" Slap! "Back of the class, make sure that you stand" "No break for you" (except that of your heart)... You drew your stars differently right from the start.

You held it all in like an overfull bin. You cried on your own as emotions were never shown to the dangerous grownups you could be thrown, "You must have done something wrong, adults are always right, off you go now, run along, get out of my sight". "Just do what you're told and don't ever be bold". And so, it went on until you were grown. An un-nurtured blossom, you grew tall on your own, as they sniggered and laughed all through your teens, the lethal princesses, the ruthless queens. Your friends were not genuine, they suited themselves, you were good for a day, then back on the shelves. "You are far too sensitive", "I was only joking" You took the brunt of relentless criticism endlessly spoken. You hid your true self, your wild spirit unbroken, your life deemed unimportant, just a valueless token...You drew your stars differently right from the start.

You wanted to belong, to be 'normal', to fit in, "Who do you think you are? You can never join in". Your gifts of kindness and caring were often abused, yet never considered valid currency to be used. Not even to gain access as a payment or bribe, to enlist or belong to any special tribe. Voices echoed, "Do what you're told now, be a good girl", "She's difficult, that one, with the stubborn cropped hair (which refused to uncurl). "Don't be yourself or make any trouble", "If you are very lucky some man will marry you, so don't burst that bubble". Men and boys were the thing, doing sports, maths, and science. Girls became housewives without a word of defiance. With women of your era there was no great alliance, no standing together in oppositional triumph. No positive roles, no inspirational female leaders, the times were so different, most women became subservient pleasers. You knew all along that this way was so wrong, but you still had no voice yet, could not sing your song... You drew your stars differently right from the start.

Deep in your soul, you held on to your essence, safely invisible to those who disparaged your presence. You knew who you were from the moment of your conception; all the while you were waiting and watching for signs of insurrection. You bid your time well and bathed in the light of beautiful rainbows that would help you take flight. To be touched by a rainbow was considered an extra blow – "What a waste; she will never be perfect you know", "What to do with the likes of you? Keep your flaws well hidden, make sure they don't show"... You drew your stars differently right from the start.

As an amazing CREATRIX there were no plans for your career, you nourished yourself and overcame insidious fear. You placed your feet into brand new shoes, stepped forward bravely kicking aside all that felt false or untrue. Living tenaciously with sovereignty intact was your self-guiding principle, your unique pact, as you emerged victoriously to live your best life so gloriously. You created a beautiful home with your partner/lover, who stood by your side on your long journey to recover, an equal in all, who nurtured your talents. Life was good and wholly in balance. With new parenting skills overcoming many ills, raising a wonderful family in kindness and devotion, unconditional love with no drama or commotion, the past mistakes would never repeat. An honour and a privilege to recognise your daughters as complete... You drew your stars differently right from the start.

Neuro-divergent was a phrase you had not before heard, until it came into your awareness when your own young child was given these words. Testing, assessing with full diagnosis, support and assistance, a positive plan, an empowering prognosis. Now your own hidden issues were finally discovered, unawareness, dormant for decades, finally uncovered. Considered for too long a misfit, an odd bird, redemption then freed you of all labels incurred. It all made such sense now; you no longer needed to dwell in a place of past tense. Different, individual, distinctive, not part of any common flock, you had been revealed as a rare precious bird, you took time to take stock, a true Rainbow Being in every sense of the word... You drew your stars differently right from the start.

Your life's anthem of choice was stirring and bodacious, no longer accepting anything sexist or salacious. Gloria's voice was all up in your head, "Wake up now woman, your soul is not dead! "Rise up girl and do your thing, you are a great survivor and now you can sing in the chant of a winner, a warrior, a queen, "I WILL SURVIVE". It was no longer a dream. Gloria Gaynor's song had lyrics that resonated, a woman standing strong who would not be eradicated... You drew your stars differently right from the start.

You embody it all now, rising up to any challenge or task, you are mighty and triumphant, a Goddess without a mask. You are wrapped in a majestic cloak of full rainbow spectrum, red, orange, yellow, green, blue, indigo and violet, your past existence, your self-preservation and determination, acknowledgements, a wondrous credit. You have discarded all remnants of the once colourless shroud, shaking loose your massive unshorn curls on your head held high and proud... You drew your stars differently right from the start.

Here in the now you embrace your uniqueness, encouraging others to value all gifts they possess. You are dynamic, a free thinker, your imagination runs riot, so how could they ever have instructed YOU to be quiet? You are now uncontainable as you step into your stride, your stance is so purposeful and your 'reach' far and wide. For you, the box to think outside has been folded away neatly, without fuss or tears, no one cried. You are a free, independent woman and so wonderfully wild... You drew your stars differently right from the start and they have remained your one constant to guide your pure heart. They shine above you in all your worldly endeavours; they will illuminate your distinctive perspective forever and ever. Using a full palette of rich vibrant colour to adorn the Rainbow Goddess as your nurturing mother, you passionately sing out to all other rainbow beings around, to create their own drawings in colourful abound..." Scribble the star shapes on your luminous skin to draw out the magical incandescent stardust that lies deep within". Draw your stars differently right from the start.

May 2022

She Drew Her Stars Differently Right from the Start

Barbara O'Meara

Mixed Media Acrylic on Canvas

Sensitive

Geneviève Labonté

I was that little girl,
bothered by tags on clothes,
and seams on socks,
thrown off by strong scents
and loud noises;
a picky eater,
who liked only the blandest
and sweetest of tastes.

I was the young girl
with a narrow range of comfort:
sweater on, sweater off
sweater on, sweater off
easily too cold, easily too hot–
my senses turned up high.
I was always the last to fall asleep
at sleep overs,
and the first to wake up
at any little sound.

I was the girl,
who before I even knew
what puberty was,
was used as a stand in
blow up doll
for a teenage boy
wanting to practice making out.
Did I mention
that he hated me
with a vengeance?

Add hypervigilance
to an already turned up
sensory system.

I was the hypervigilant,
hypersensitive teen,
wanting to go with the flow,
but physically unable.

An Autistic Bibliophile's Tale

Jessica Penot

I once went back and found my first journal. I was 5 when I wrote it. In it, I said I wanted to be a "riter of bocs". Even when I was 5, the only thing I wanted was to write. I knew that the only thing that ever made me happy were stories and books. I wanted to be lost in books. I wanted to be lost in words and in stories. I wanted to dive so deep into fantasy worlds that I wouldn't ever have to come up for breath. The real world was too terrifying. Nothing in it ever made sense. Everyone was always mad at me. I never did anything right. From the time I was very young, I felt like I didn't belong to anything. I was a puzzle piece put in the wrong box. I was difficult. I was a disappointment. When I wrote and read, however, I could be whoever I wanted and in books, I found other heroes and heroines who felt as out of place as I did. Books were the world that made sense to me.

I wrote my first novel on my mother's old typewriter when I was 11 years old. It was a tragic thing. It was so influenced by Anne Rice it felt like a bad copy of Anne Rice, but her novels spoke to me as a child. I could relate more to the vampires wandering the world searching for some glimpse of humanity than I could to my peers. Those vampires with their lonely lives of isolation felt like kindred spirits. Real people were enigmas. I tried to interact with them. I desperately wanted to be like them. I wanted friends, I wanted attachment, but people never made sense. I knew I was always acting wrong and upsetting them, but beyond that, I had no idea what they expected of me or what motivated their behavior. So, I wrote my first novel. I created a space where the main character could make beauty from her strangeness, where she could find solace in her isolation. I made a world for myself where I belonged. In the pages of my book, my strange and lonely heroine could find love and friendship. She could find acceptance where none had ever been available to me.

Writing and reading remained my life for years, but in college I turned away from the English degree, as I wanted to pursue a degree that was a little more practical. So, I became a psychologist. Despite my career change, I didn't change. I couldn't fit in with the normal. Oddly, as a therapist I could connect with people. I could understand them and maybe because I felt so isolated, I worked harder than most therapists to make sure none of my clients ever did, but connection was lost to me. So, I wrote and read. All my characters were isolated and born different. They were born witches, born gods, born demons, but there was always some reason why no matter how hard they tried, they could never fit in or be understood by normal humanity.

I worked out my isolation behind computer screens. I wrote about a psychologist who lived alone in a haunted house in Alabama. She was born a witch and the only way she could find help for her clients was to embrace her true nature and turn to witchcraft. I wrote about a warrior on a distant world who was born different and the only way they could find peace was to embrace their true nature. The same theme repeated, but I never understood why. I didn't know I had autism. I knew I felt alone, but I didn't understand.

By the time I was 40 I had published 10 books. I still had my psychology practice, but I had a mountain of failed friendships and relationships behind me. My otherness remained as distinct and well-marked upon me as Hester Prim's Scarlet Letter. I might as well have had "freak: avoid at all costs" tattooed to my forehead. When I was finally diagnosed with autism, things began to finally make sense.

The last book I wrote was *Jane of Air*. It was a young adult retelling of my favorite book, *Jane Eyre*. It was told with a bit of a Lovecraftian twist so that Jane was born with a tattoo of a door on her back. She was smart and beautiful but different and off-putting and as she aged the tattoo grew and changed. It became larger. The bones of the story were like the story of *Jane Eyre*, but ghosts and old gods littered the hallways of Thornfield Hall and Jane herself was an unsmiling intellectual who spoke wrong and looked wrong. People moved away from her. She didn't know what to do with her face and loud noises and odd foods could send her running. All of this was because she was born with part of an old god in her. She was born different. She couldn't change it. She could see she was part monster, but she lacked the ability to be human, despite her desperate desire to belong. I didn't know I was autistic when I wrote this book, but I knew Jane was me. I knew I felt like a monster. I felt like an outsider. I felt like I was born different and no matter how hard I tried to cover up who I really was, in the end people always found out and when they found out, they ran away.

I always knew all my characters were me. They were lost and broken and so different from humanity that they always feel almost doomed from the start. They don't know how to connect or relate to the world, and they are desperately grasping for love and connection in any form. They are odd and other people avoid them. They try to pretend to be like everyone else, but they always fall short.

I spent my entire life falling short, being left out. I would make friendships and they would fade and die. Something always went wrong. I knew it was me. Even this year, I made a group of female friends who understood I had autism and when I allowed my mask to fall too far down, they all ran away. The lesson was as clear as it was when I was 10. I was wrong. The way I relate and respond to the world isn't appropriate. It is weird and I am to be avoided. I was diagnosed with autism a little over a year ago. I lack self-awareness and struggle with alexithymia so even as I could see autism in my clients and could assess and diagnose it accurately, I couldn't see it in myself. I had treated autism and done autism assessments for five years before I realized I had autism and had myself assessed.

It was only when I read an article in *Neuroclastic* about Jane Eyre as the first autistic heroine that I began to see the parallels in my life. I realized that all my characters were autistic. All their burdens were symbolic representations for what it feels like to be born autistic. According to Leedham et al (2015), findings suggest that women prior to diagnosis feel powerless and broken and after diagnosis they get an increased sense of agency. After my diagnosis, I experienced this. I saw all my female characters as myself and I realized that their only path to freedom was accepting their inner monsters, my only path was accepting mine. I had to accept my autism and embrace it. I had to love it for what it was and mourn that it had taken from me.

The last book I read was *Circe* by Madeline Miller. It is the story of the lonely witch who seduced Ulysses. As I read this book, I related to Circe more than to any neurotypical person. Circe was exiled to live alone on an island because she was so exceedingly different from the other gods and nymphs. She struggles through her entire existence to find peace with this. She gets angry. She turns men into pigs. She fights gods, but in the end, the only path to peace is to accept she can't be like the other gods. She must embrace who she is. No matter how many times I read and write this story of the isolated woman who has to learn she can't be like the others, I still struggle to accept it. Because for me, being autistic has been learning to accept that I will be the lonely witch on the island. Learning to accept that I will be isolated, but in that isolation, there is great beauty. And that beauty and strength beyond measure can be found if I can only accept that my witchcraft lies in books and my magic can only be truly understood if I embrace my solitude.

Divine Creatrix

Arna Baartz

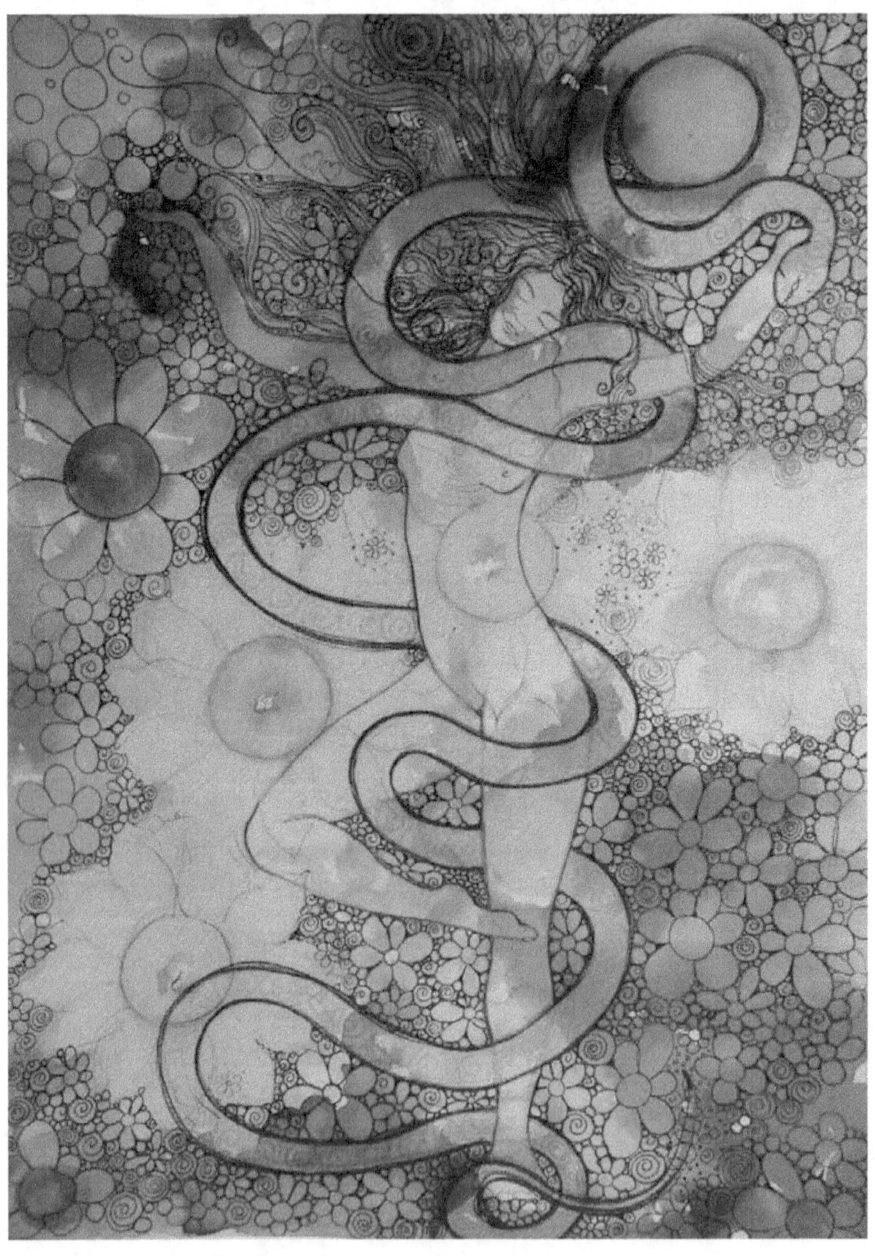

Creatrix, part 1

Molly Remer

Sometimes creativity
is a fire I can't make space for,
a demand I'm not big enough
to fulfill,
a battering wave,
an endless tower,
a full-blast faucet
of uncontrollable inspiration.
It crumbles my human limits,
believes in miracles,
and refuses to be silenced,
clawing its way madly
from the bent lines
and wild constraints
of a human-sized life
and demanding to be heard
and held,
asking,
always asking,
to be so much MORE,
ravenous for time,
starving for silence,
and ragged with need.
It is sharp-edged and fierce,
ferocious and tenacious,
worn at the edges
and molten at the core.

Creatrix, part 2

Molly Remer

Sometimes creativity
feels like an insatiable mistress,
a fire of passion
that flares up
to consume
all parts
of a human-sized life.
She asks for everything
and often
just
a
little bit
more.
Sometimes I feel small
and ashen
in the center,
my fingers bravely clasping
the trailing ends
of so many spiraling
and wild threads.
May I remember that
I am the fire,
I am the center,
I am the wild,
I am the threads.

Reaching for the Stars

Barbara O'Meara

Acrylic on Canvas

Attention Surplus/Half an Hour in the Life of a Neurodivergent Mother

Jenny Beech

'I was referred to the psychiatrist more than six months ago, has there been any progress with my referral? *We don't have your name, you need to call the psychiatry department their number is- you'll have to ring the main reception for appointments- have you got a pen?* Do I have a pen? Where are the pens? I swear there was one there yesterday. That's the number for the psychiatry department, they sent me to you- *call the mental health team, ask for Heather- that's your local mental health nurse, call the surgery-* but that's where I started?- *you missed a call two months ago-*

Voices. Snippets of song. Flashing images.

Hello, this is Heather. Is now a good time to talk? Fuck. Stop crying. It's okay, take your time. On a scale of one to ten, how would you describe your mood?

I asked for my blood results so I could take them to the next appointment. Then I forgot, again and again and a few more times. Then I remembered. I don't know where I put them. Did I lose that jewelry, or was it stolen? Is she stealing from me? Maybe I'm remembering wrong? But I'm never remembering wrong. I forget, but I don't remember wrong. Not that anyone believes me.

Is she stealing from me?

I wrote a list. I wrote it in my notebook. Where's my notebook? Upstairs. Upstairs. Kettle's still on. I'll only be quick. That reminds me, must put a wash on. I'll do that now. Would that be colours or darks? Mustn't forget the kid's clothes. Hang on, they don't have any clean clothes. *Really* mustn't forget the kid's clothes. How did this room get messy? I'll just put that away. And that. And that. Need to keep on top of it. Now what was I...?

Washing. What's that noise? The kettle! Downstairs. Quicker. Turn off the hob. Ouch! Why is that hot? Did I put two hobs on? Right, now- washing. It's in a pile on the landing. Wait- cup of tea. I'm thirsty. Shit, I'm thirsty. Did I drink anything today? No. What's the time? Two o'clock?! I'll pour the tea first. What was that noise? Where are the kids? I'll just check.

All fine.

Mum?

They're happy playing.

Mum?

I'll pour the tea first. I'm thirsty.

Mum!

Did someone call me?

Mum!

Yes, Sweetheart? Yes, you can get out the colouring, that's fine. Thanks for asking.

Tea. Tea. Cup of tea. I'll sit down to drink it. I'll just pop the washing in while it brews. Upstairs. Hold on.

Frozen mid-step.

I've forgotten something. Just pick that up. Washing, washing, washing. There we are. Back downstairs. Washing in. Teabag out, milk in. That smells good. Gosh, I'm thirsty.

Mum?

Yes, Sweetheart? Oh, the pens should be in the cupboard. I'll come help you look. Is that my alarm? Where's my phone? That sounds like it's upstairs. I'll be right back, sweetheart.

Alarm- *deadline.*

Deadline? Deadline for what?! Was that for last week?

Mum!

Sorry, Sweetheart. Pens. There they are. I think the paper's in your room.

Did I switch the washing machine on? I'll just check. What does 'deadline' mean? Was it important? Should I call Him to see if He remembers? I'll call him anyway. He's so nice to talk to.

Fuck. TEA.

I'll call him and sit down with my tea. Why is the tea cold? I'll re-heat it. Where's the little pan? Maybe I should get a microwave.

Hob back on. Nope, that's the wrong one, try again. There we are.

I didn't check the washing machine. It's too quiet.

The washing machine isn't on. I left the dog outside! Oh dear.

Sorry, Girl. I forgot you were out there.

Did I forget the laundry liquid? I'll put more in, just in case. What's that doing there? I'll just put that away. My keys! Best put them in the front door before I forget, or I'll never remember where they are.

Mummy?

It's a bit chilly. Is there a door open somewhere? I didn't close it after the dog came in! No wonder it's cold, I'll just go- nope- keys. Keys in front door first. Cold breeze. Must close that back door. No! Put the keys in the lock, you'll lose them if you- where's that breeze coming from? Oh, the back door is open- NO! KEYS!

Turns to front door. Turns around. Takes one step. Turns around. Swivels back and forth like a puppy playing piggy in the middle.

Mummy?

Put the keys in the door. There we are.

Let's close that backdoor. All the heat's gone now. Did someone say my name?

Yes, Lovely? Of course, you can have a cuddle. Why don't we have a cuddle while I ring Daddy and drink my- fuck! Tea.

It's boiled over. It tastes disgusting when it's boiled over. I'll start again.

Right. Kettle on. Yes, Lovely? Sure, I'll get you some milk.

Did I forget-?

Turns around.

No! Stay put! Drink your tea! That's what he says- 'Drink your tea!'

I should get that on a t-shirt. There you are Lovely, there's your milk.

Watch the kettle. It's nice the way it boils and bubbles in there. It's a nice sound. Like rain on a roof. Only the rain is trying to get out rather than in. All those little atoms jumping and buzzing just to make me a cup of-

How long has that been boiling? Never mind. Turn it off. Water in mug. Tea bag in mug. Wait. I'll just go and tidy-

No! Wait, woman. Fucking tea.

That looks strong enough. Milk. Tea bag out. Smells delicious. Sit down. I'll just give him a call.

Does anyone want to talk to Daddy?

(Faintly) *'No!'*

'Hello, my love. How's your day going?'

*'*Not bad. I can't seem to focus on...'

Waxwork Child

Helen Langdon

You stand outside the classroom
Lips pursed, shutters down
A waxwork of yourself.
From hour to hour, many teachers buzz around
Perplexed
Is it me? They want to know. Assume your silence personal.
I become your shield
Your voice
Before you melt.
Your twelve long years hang heavy on your shoulders.
I coax, cajole
You'll be fine once you're inside, I say
And sometimes I break through –
The threshold crossed.
A small victory in my humble role
With its precarious power.
And once inside you'd talk for hours
About the books you read
A different child.
And later once the teacher's voice becomes a blur I walk around
and see
The websites
Autism
ADHD
Contraband – the lesson's task is out of hand
My grasp is slipping.
And yet
And yet
I understand
In ways you'll never know.

But here and now
I'm here
And fear I don't have long
Before you're wax once more.

She Who Shouts the Loudest

Beth Rees

Growing up, I was always teased for being a chatterbox. For constantly talking and not listening, for interrupting others when they spoke, for talking excessively about my favourite books, a keen interest in World War II and how I wanted to be a vet when I grew up. I talked AT people, not TO them. I was embarrassed about it but couldn't stop the words from propelling out of my mouth. What I didn't know was that 30 years later, I would find out why and that it wasn't my fault.

I could never keep a secret

On many an occasion, I have been known to ruin surprises. My undiagnosed neurodiverse brain didn't understand why I needed to pretend not to know something when I did. The rules were confusing, and many birthday and Christmas surprises were accidentally revealed. My parents' favourite story is about the first time I met my (now) stepdad. When he pulled up to our cosy semi-detached house for the first time, my little sister and I were playing in the cul-de-sac outside. He emerged from the car with a big, beautiful, bouquet of flowers for mum. He introduced himself and asked if mum was at home. Without hesitation, I ran off down the driveway and fell through the front door yelling, "Mum! He's here... And he brought flowers!" Bam went that surprise. For the next 20 years, I talked his ears off about everything and anything, not letting him get a word in sideways, edgeways, or anyways.

"She talks too much and doesn't listen."

I tended to take over conversations and thought listening was an inconvenience, so sometimes, I just tuned out.

Both "She talks too much in class" and "she doesn't listen" appeared various times in my school reports. Teachers would comment on how exceptional my English studies were but my maths and science lagged behind. For some reason, the numbers never made sense. When I came home from school with maths homework, I would melt down and cry hysterically because I didn't understand. I was always better at the arts than subjects involving numbers. I guess that's why no one ever twigged that I might be autistic. I put my excessive chatter to good use and studied drama, which I was really good at. Standing up in front of a crowd and pretending to be someone else came easily. That's all I wished for as a kid. That I was someone else. Someone cooler. Someone less weird. Someone who didn't talk so much that it annoyed everyone. I felt like I was on a different wavelength than other people. I masked who I was and playing fictional characters helped me to perfect the art of hiding the real me. I was an A* student in drama and did it outside of school too. People seemed to like the confident and extroverted me they saw in plays and I felt like, for once, I fit in somewhere.

Great at job interviews…

My chameleon-like abilities helped when I talked my way into a public relations career. My fiancé, to this day, says that I'm really good at interviews. They didn't faze me and still don't because I see them as another acting role. I continued to tell myself "If you are confident, curious, creative and courageous, people will like you better." I managed to bag myself a lot of jobs which was great. Until I realized, I actually had to work as advertised.

That is when things fell apart. There were some instances I couldn't talk my way out of.

Being late for work, being unable to multitask, unable to cope with bright and busy workspaces, not understanding colleague sarcasm or cruelty and not being able to do the job I said I could. I couldn't meet deadlines (which I now know is because I'm totally time blind), organise my work, break focus when something needed doing ASAP, and being rude to colleagues and clients when I felt criticised. Most days, I would go home and cry, putting myself on mute to save further humiliation. I couldn't speak, even if I wanted to. The words were trapped in my throat and refused to move.

One failed job turned into another. And another. And another. Considering I worked in communications, my communication was failing me. It was like everyone knew I was a phony and picked me apart until I cracked. I couldn't talk to family or friends because what would I say? I told them I was brilliant at public relations but turns out, I'm not and now they think I lied. Oh yeah, and I've been fired again.

"You're just a square peg in a round hole."

It was after one such event that I sat with my stepdad in tears saying, 'I don't fit in. I can't do what everyone else is doing. My brain is stupid. I'm stupid. I hate myself."

Through awkward hugs (I always find hugs awkward but again, now I know why), he said, "You're just a square peg in a round hole. You just haven't found your place yet. But you will." His kind and wise words gave me reassurance, but deep down I felt like an imposter, talking myself into a career that clearly, wasn't made for me. However, I persevered. I might've felt like a failure but I'm not a quitter.

"You have borderline personality disorder (BPD)."

During one of my more recent job roles, I experienced a catastrophic breakdown, crying uncontrollably, rocking back and forth, unable to communicate. I'd lost my voice again. The words wouldn't come – meaning that my fiancé had to talk to medical professionals on my behalf. After seeing a psychiatrist, they diagnosed me with borderline personality disorder (BPD) – a mood condition affecting how people see and think about the world. I was confused and upset. Was this the reason I'd found life so hard? Because my personality was 'disordered'? After reading about BPD, I felt even more confused. What I read did not seem like me. It was only when I spoke about the diagnosis with my counsellor, that she strongly disagreed.

"I don't think you have BPD. I'm positive you're autistic."

She told me that she didn't agree with the BPD diagnosis. Instead, she was convinced I was autistic. This took me completely by surprise. Autism? No one had ever suggested that to me. I voiced my confusion and she said, "You present in many of the same ways as me and I'm autistic."

Once again, I was left speechless.

She encouraged me to read more into it, take an AQ Test and see if I could be assessed by the local health service. I became all consumed by my research, reading and self-testing. That's when I realised she might be right. I tried to get an appointment with a psychiatrist to review my BPD diagnosis and they told me to 'stop being so dramatic' and told me firmly 'We won't be assessing you for autism because you're not autistic. You have a mental health condition which we are treating.'

End of conversation.

Why won't anyone listen?

In the years that followed, I tried to use my voice to get a medical person to listen, but they wouldn't. Between 2017 and 2020, I'd had five jobs, one of which was directly impacted by the debated diagnosis and the 800mg of antipsychotic drugs they put me on to 'control my mania and delusions' (neither of which I ever had). I reached breaking point and in November 2020, a psychiatrist finally told me that the diagnosis was wrong and that she thought I was autistic and had ADHD.

My counsellor was right all along. My gut was right too.

I burst into tears of frustration and relief, hoping things would change. But they didn't. She wouldn't diagnose me as autistic with ADHD, but she also wouldn't take the BPD misdiagnosis away. I was stuck in limbo for a year waiting for an autism assessment. On strong medication I didn't need, for a mental health condition I never had.

Self-diagnosed autism – "Is that a thing?"

After the initial depression, I spoke with my counsellor again. She was outraged but let me know that, while I was waiting for my autism assessment, I could 'self-diagnose.' This definitely confused me.

"I thought only medical professionals or those trained could diagnose autism?"

She said, "That's true. However, self-diagnosis is used in the autistic community because of how difficult it is to get a formal diagnosis. The criteria are so outdated and exclude so many genders, races, and communities, it's hard for people to be diagnosed. It's more identification than diagnosis and is accepted."

As soon as I came off the phone, I looked into it and realised that self-diagnosis could help me with my assessment at the end of 2021. It meant that I'd be able to understand myself better and work out what I could do to help myself until assessment day came.

Using my voice to cope.

So, I got back into chatterbox mode and decided now was the time to use my voice. Now was the time to shout from the rooftops about my experience and how medically, they'd got it wrong. How they'd ignored my pleas and put it down to being 'dramatic' and 'attention seeking' and how I was having to 'self-diagnose' until I was assessed. I began making Instagram reels about my experiences and soon realised that it wasn't just me going through this. There were hundreds of other people doing this too. Hundreds of other confused and misplaced people who just wanted to be understood. After my first few videos, I received lots of messages from females saying that they 'felt seen.' They thought they were alone in their experiences and felt better knowing they weren't.

By sharing my story, I unknowingly gave voice to what turned out to be thousands of other people, mainly women aged between 20–70, struggling to be recognised or heard by the diagnostic system. Throughout 2021, we shared our experiences, gave comfort to one another, and helped each other cope with a process that many of us would never experience and get answers from.

In December 2021, I was finally diagnosed as autistic with ADHD. My emotions were all over the place. Relief. Frustration. Confusion. Satisfaction. That was until the health service refused to acknowledge the diagnoses. Once again, I used my voice but this time, I kept in mind, 'She who shouts the loudest' gets heard. It resulted in a meeting with a manager and director of the health board who had no idea that my diagnoses weren't being taken seriously. They were also horrified to hear that my medical records hadn't been changed to reflect the diagnoses.

I confidently told them that this same scenario was playing out for other women who were given mental health diagnoses they didn't have because no one wanted to admit they might be autistic or have ADHD and need support. Finally, my voice had actually been heard, acknowledged, and appreciated, not shut down, drowned out or ignored.

Don't be afraid to use your voice.

What I want you to know, lovely reader, is that even though I am a next-level chatterbox, using my voice wasn't always easy. But it was necessary. Sometimes you have to dig deep to find the words that will ultimately change your life. If you can't verbalise them, write them down and share them with loved ones and if you feel you can, medical professionals too.

Just because we're female, it doesn't mean we should be ignored. We deserve to be helped and feel empowered to be the people we really, truly are.

Undiagnosed
Schuyler Witman

When I am alone
among others
I beat my drum
but I am still not in the band
When I am alone among others
I sometimes walk
And the names of my friends
blossom on my tongue
    Wild Carrot
                Dock
                     Thistle
      Hawthorn
                  Clover
                        Morning Glory

Each familiar face
invites me out, invites me in
So I lean in close
to a stranger
"Do I know you?
What is your name?"
For a moment I forget myself
and we are the song

Mother Spiral, Seed of Life
Experiencing Dyscalculia

Claire Dorey

"Like a circle in a spiral, like a wheel within a wheel
Never ending or beginning on an ever spinning reel
As the images unwind, like the circles that you find
In the windmills of your mind!"

- *The Windmills of Your Mind* - Songwriters: Marilyn Bergman, Michel Legrand and Alan Bergman.

A page becomes a prison when you are judged by your ability to decipher what is written on it. Perpendicular walls bearing down. Clock. Chair. Desk. SOS. Amy struggles with numbers. Never ending or beginning, equations unwind, in the turbines of her mind. She simply doesn't speak their language.

Long division became her long disintegration, a slow unravelling. Minute hand passing hours, weeks, years staring at reems of algebra, a feedback loop of maths overwhelm, a cycle of apprehension and forgetting. Frustration. Confusion. Clock. Chair. Desk. SOS. Page blank. Mind blank. Anxiety. Freeze. Eventually Amy shuts down. She sinks to the bottom of the sea and stays there.

She learns how to hide behind her failure in the same way she hides behind her hair. Failure weaves itself into her future. She is the girl trapped in the spider web, invalidated, stigmatised, blemished, labelled as lazy and simple, a crooked tooth on a cog, in a system that requires uniformity.

Capitalist patriarchy is a dangerous place for little girls. It erodes their confidence and makes them question themselves. When a child shuts down it's really hard to get them back. Shut down. A default setting. Imagine a fragile flower growing on stony ground, unable to thrive.

Five years later Amy did what any self-respecting teenager would do. She rebelled. She threw her pen across the floor. That was it! Amy had expressed herself! No one noticed the broken pen. No one noticed the shy girl struggling at the back, in silence, for years. Amy struggled with Dyscalculia. Dysrhythmia. Mathslexia. Number Dyslexia. Maths Blindness. She wasn't Dyslexic. She wasn't simple. She had a difficulty learning maths. Fractions eluded her.

Confidence corroding. Clock. Chair. Desk. SOS.

A page becomes a prison when what is written on it defines your future. It seems incredible that something you failed at as a child should continue to dictate the opportunities that are open to you as an adult. Why are we all judged by the same scale? In this hostile patriarchal system, human units pass along the production line, a conveyor belt of conformity, to quality control, where they are rubber-stamped for worthiness, quirks, diversity, and individuality abandoned! Are there any certificates for the endurance, resilience, and resourcefulness of the rainbow child survivor?

We are all children of the Universe. There is a system that is much more powerful than patriarchy – the system of Mother Nature, the mother of manifestation. Her divine spark – the Divine Feminine, source of healing, intuition and light – is within all of us! In Mother Nature you can stumble and sink to the bottom of the ocean and find inspiration there.

There were pages that enthralled and captivated Amy. A circle within a spiral, she sought refuge in the pages of novels, sketch books and journals, where her imagination ran free. In books she went on wild, imaginary adventures and when she grew up, she travelled to the places her curiosity had led her to. Mother Nature welcomed her and gave her the space to breathe, under a vast expansive sky. A circle dilating in a spiral, like a pupil in an eye, wide-eyed, she unlearned her conditioning and connected to the wonder of the universe, seeking joy by observing the small things.

Perhaps the story of how and why we humans became units, to be quantified and commodified, can be explained by the story of the rise of patriarchy, man's divorce from nature.

On her travels, her journey back to the Goddess within, Amy grew to understand how our ancestors viewed mathematics as being key to the secrets of the universe but for them it was a communal act that was embedded in Mother Nature. They dragged huge boulders across the landscape and used them to build circles within circles to measure the cycles of the sky dome. They held huge festivals. Everyone was welcome. No one sat isolated, staring at oblivion, whilst a clock marked time.

In the wilds of Angelsey, she cut open an apple and observed how the seeds form a pentagram. The spirit of the Druids informed her that when she ate that apple, she was consuming its wisdom. It was there, with the sea breeze tugging at her hair, that Amy realised that maths could be an animist science, not separate from the life force of the natural world that vibrates all around us!

In the foothills of Crete, she tasted the sweet elixir of honey straight from the hive and the beekeeper gave her a piece of hexagonal honeycomb. Amongst the wildflowers she learnt how our ancestors honoured the bees as Goddess, whose geometry was woven into the biosphere.

In the moonlight, on a beach in Brazil she watched turtles hatch and noticed that there are 28 segments around the edge of a turtle's shell, one for each day in the lunar month. There are thirteen hexagons in the centre of the shell, one for each moon cycle. The geometry of creation that is entwined with the cycles of the cosmos also dictates the rhythms women flow to, wheels within wheels. With the tide lapping her toes, Amy realised that the mysterious force within the fractal multiverse is Mother Nature.

In the mountain villages of Morocco, she witnessed how artisans treat maths as a visual science. She watched weavers working at the loom, intuitively remembering complex codes, handed down through the generations, that were never written down. These visual codes form patterns and motifs that tell stories and preserve histories. Woven into textiles, worn as garments and for rugs in the home, this coding is infused into domestic life, cocooning, and decorating the community, rather than being used as a device to grade and alienate individuals.

In India she chanted OHM, the sound of the universe and learnt how our ancestors understood cymatics, the geometry of sound and in Egypt she sang in temples that were built to resonate.

In a museum in Germany, she was drawn to a stone statue of three female deities, seated in a line. The spirit of these deities spoke to her how the sacred numbers 3, 6 and 9 are an integral part of the cosmic blueprint. For example, a circle has 360 degrees, a right angle has 90 degrees, and a triangle has three sides. Surrounded by millennia of historical artifacts, it became clear why the ancestors honoured these numbers in the form of the Triple Goddess.

"If you only knew the magnificence of the 3, 6 and 9 you would have a key to the universe." - Nikola Tesla.

Mother Spiral, Seed of Life, Tree of Knowledge – when sacred maths relate to the patterns and consciousness embodied in the natural world, Amy can easily understand these principles. It's just the number coding that baffles her! So why is she judged on it?

Stop the clocks. Wind back time 5,000 years. There's an error in the system. It's time to end this long season of forgetting and remember the insidious rise of male-biased, top-down hierarchy and expose its history of obsessively grading, measuring, and commodifying humans... to control them. Let's end the system of not feeling good enough, that we have all got used to. Let's abandon power structures reliant on the myth of the sovereign head, the musty old pontiff, the tormentor, the feeble patrician, the rogue man god, the power seekers, the prestige hunters, the judgement passers.

Haunted by the ghosts of trauma, rupturing adults, burdened by shame, make the long migration back to their broken inner child so they can heal. The road to self-acceptance is a tough one in dominator societies that bypass empathy. Why cut the roots before the tree has grown? Why clip the wings before the bird has flown? Why do we accept the damage structural hierarchy does to us, where we are all so alone?

Fast forward time! Let's build a future where everyone's needs are catered for, including Mother Nature. Let's open schools of self-worth, where tuning into creative wisdom and intuition is part of normal life. Let's shift the narrative to one of patience, nurture, cooperation, and acceptance that a matrifocal community can provide – a listening circle within the Circle of Life!

We are all circles in a spiral, a kaleidoscope of miracles, as complete as a circle, as expansive as the spiral, waiting to exhale. Let's spiral back to our centre, to the sacred dimension we all have within ourselves, the quiet space, free from distraction and judgement, where we can open our hearts. There we can create the space to process a whirlwind of thoughts, some radiant, some toxic, some to hang on to, some to let go, an ever-spinning wheel. Breathe in. Breathe out. Let go!

Let's plant a forest for Mother Nature, an antidote to a world that is spinning too quickly. Let's all slow down, rest our nervous systems and shelter beneath the wise old branches of the World Tree.

Every story has an ending and a beginning and another ending and another beginning, a season within a season, a wheel within a wheel, an out breath and an in breath. Every seed has potential. Retrieve your soul and fly.

SOS. Mama Earth knows best!

Art by Claire Dorey

References

Neurodiversity and Co-occurring difficulties: Dyscalculia and maths difficulties, British Dyslexia Association.

Uncontained

Molly Remer

I often feel as if I have to quell the inspiration,
tamp down the motivation,
quiet the creations,
soothe the fire that burns within
to do and be and move and make.
I hold myself back
because otherwise
I overwhelm and exhaust myself
use myself up,
leaving only that which is parched
and threadbare
quivering on the edge.
How would it feel to be unrestricted,
unleashed,
unrestrained,
no longer consciously quieted,
sometimes forcibly stilled.
Would I tire out
or would I fly?
I do not know
because I can never truly
let myself be fully uncontained,
filling the corners
of my own life
and expanding past the edges
into the unknown beyond.

Quitting

Molly Remer

I am calling it quits
on this nonsense.
I'm retiring from
the reminding and the finding,
stopping the striving,
shutting down the service,
hanging a closed sign
over the doorway to my time.
I'm letting it all rest,
undone, unfinished,
cockeyed, and full of typos.
I'm daring to disappoint,
hopping off the treadmill
of performing and pleasing
and earning love through action.
I'm finished, y'all,
turning off the flow
and going to bed,
I'm shutting down
the stream that bleeds from my heart
into the abyss of need.
I'm stepping in to letting others down,
so that I might actually discover
how to live again,
fully here,
in my own skin.

What if I could learn that it is possible
to do all this disappointing
and expectation shearing,
and yet,
still come out alive and breathing,
blinking into the sunshine
and finding out there's
a rainbow underneath
all those clouds
I've been carrying in my arms.

Apothecary

Sylvia Bhagavati

Radical Ideas for Living

Molly Remer

If you need to eat something,
do so and let it nourish you.
If you need to drink something,
do so and let it refill you.
If you need to rest,
do so and let it restore you.
If you need to create something
do so, and let it replenish you.
You are worthy of me, truth,
trust, and tenderness.
Let it in.

The Rainbows of Life on The Journey Home

Deborah A. Meyerriecks

A funny thing happened on the way to here. I got sidetracked. I found someplace new. I put words to feelings and experiences that never had words to them for me before and in the perfection of what they express, I accept them as my truth. Previously unspoken words now flow freely. Like the crystal prism made from water drops. Unexpected and gone without witness if care is not taken to follow the freshness of falling rain and bubbling creek.

I made a social media post about something completely unrelated and in that moment, it completely related. I even tagged Trista and let her know that with a whole week before the May 1st call for submission deadline, I may have something to write about. Trust me when I say, a week is a lifetime even though it's a wave whose potential could often lift me up and set me back down while I watch the potential ride flow closer to the shore without me. Often in the comfortable, free floating of existing without schedule, time undulates around me while I feel in stasis.

I was already at my laptop. I had a topic. It was perfect for a Rainbow Goddess with undiagnosed ADHD who is often frozen with Executive Dysfunction. I need a spark to release a little serotonin and release enough adrenaline so that I can keep focus on task and get it done. Often this means keeping focus on only the task and getting absolutely nothing else done. Unless I miss it. Then I maybe grasp the edges or the tail end and can't hold onto enough to bring a project to completion. If it's something that needs to be done, the rest is forced. It's formatted and uninspiring. It's a *have to*, not a *want to* and that almost always means incomplete. Incomplete attention, action, thoughts. Grasping for any bit of twine to tie it closed when I can't pick up the threads of inspiration to weave it together.

Or – the weaver of inspiration switched threads on me, dropped a pattern change, and what I thought I was starting finishes as a completely different project. Often very lovely even though not what I intended.

There is intention and then there is impact. When they line up together for a common purpose, the effect is satisfying in so many indescribable ways.

My other essay is beautiful. I have done the shadow work and developed the shadow care by allowing myself to dig deeply into myself and get to know her for who she actually is, and why – and to see who she's becoming. Goddess has empowered and enabled my journey. I have come to see that every pop-up class I never intended to teach was sharing new ways to deep dive into our ID in order to better understand our Ego.

I'm not broken – no matter how many people told me I was – and I began to believe it was true. I'm just wired differently. That said, it's still something that smacks me in the back of the head and across my heart much too often. Normally, I struggle to get myself organized. If I have a plan, a pathway, a destination, and a way to get there, I can write or do anything. But the planning is boring. When the subject I want to address is so all-encompassing or the destination is so vastly grand, it's difficult to narrow my view when I really want to widen it. I want to see, learn, experience, and share EVERYTHING. When I only have a free day or a couple of hours to explore – or I'm only allocated a 45-minute to 1-hour time slot to present my workshop talk – or I have a word count limit to respect, it's daunting. Too often I've let the inability to do everything restrict me from doing anything like an unseen red tape of confusion binding me still, rendering me inert.

What if I miss something I should have said? What if I travel all that way and miss the one most beautiful or meaningful insight? What if, what if, what if...? What if someone asks me what I want to have or do and in the seemingly infinite possibilities I freeze, and they think I'm not interested in doing anything so they leave on their own?

Fight, Flight, or Freeze. That freeze aspect is paralyzing.

The sharing of personal things that are really hard with people I know love me, is hard. I trust that they love me and care to hear about what's happening in my life in real time.

But in their concern, I often feel (through no fault of their own) the need to protect their feelings and reassure them I'm ok. Even when I'm not. The daunting task of remembering who told me what – of who has which current update, and whose feelings will I be hurt when I forget that I broke a personal rule against sharing personal hardships, and forgot to update them to let them know how the situation is going or if it's resolved.

Add to that the incorrect belief that my brain perversely convinces me it is absolute veracity and the emotional impermanence is heartbreaking: that when other people don't reach out to ask for updates or to just check-in and say hello, it's too easy to believe that while, yes, they are compassionate people and were genuinely concerned with my wellbeing when I shared with them how I was not ok – out of sight is out of mind. If I don't text first, they don't think of me. If they don't think of me without my initiating contact, could they even actually care? How is it possible to believe they would love me? And yes, it's a lie. It's a lie my brain tells me. Until I learned that emotional impermanence was even a thing, it was harder for me to talk myself down and out from those thoughts and feelings. When I say I could make myself cry, I mean it. I just didn't ever do it on purpose. With my Dynamic Duo (my children) and my partner, it's easy to remind myself that it isn't true. It's easy to remind myself we are all wired a bit differently. I see each of us making the effort to better understand and learn about ourselves and each other.

When I learned that this is one aspect of neurodivergency, and that it's actually normal and doesn't mean you're broken, it was empowering. It became part of my personal shadow work to see where these feelings of suddenly becoming unloved or abandoned were actually stemming from. It didn't change the way I felt in the moment. It empowered me to take charge and use those moments to explore myself at a deeper level.

The beautiful consequence is that I have opened myself to a deeper expression of myself with my goddess and learned that we are kin. I am becoming more in flow with my magick and it lets me direct it where I will, to transform my day as I choose.

The consequence of living with Rainbow Goddess energy in a neurodiverse life is needing to keep lists and calendars and set appointments and reminders. Needing to write things down in the moment, not as soon as possible. Discovering the sheer brilliance of texting memos to yourself. Talk-to-text is fast and no one else will text me from my phone number so reminders won't get lost in a string of conversations. Setting a reminder with my calendar app to keep a daily personal appointment with myself to review the previous day's texts, update and review my calendar, and look over my current to-do, to-write, to-consider lists so I can decide which is pertinent and which no longer applies.

I will never stop trying to juggle too many balls, even when I fail to remember which and how many I have up in the air. Balls we get distracted from for too long fall. I used to think that it was important to prioritize the balls (tasks and responsibilities) so you don't drop a vital one. Nora Roberts' Glass Ball Theory might be life-improving for you too. Nora describes that the mental load that is most difficult for some people is deciding which balls to drop when you have too many in the air that need constant attention. They redefine perception by suggesting you look at your balls and decide which are glass and which are plastic. Glass will shatter if you drop it, plastic won't. If you drop a plastic ball, it will bounce and you can always pick it back up later. The key is to know for yourself which of yours are glass and which are not.

Not having to give up all the things – just organize the way I think about them and how I make time to address them – is key.

Here I am, on a quiet night, a week from the first day of May. I had no commitment I would be breaking if I didn't submit anything, and earlier this week I gave myself permission to drop this ball and let it either be somewhere I could pick it up or even roll away where I wouldn't be able to find it in time to meet the deadline to submit. It was strangely more empowering than it was merely freeing. When I stopped focusing on this deadline, I made space in my head to address more urgent matters. Carrying less mental weight, I was better empowered to give my full attention to what was time sensitive this weekend. When everything that absolutely needed to be done – or the consequence would be more difficult than I would care to deal with was handled – I relaxed. I skimmed social media. I made a gratitude post. A thought was triggered. An essay was written. In review of the initial conceptual statement, I wrote for myself, I saw the first essay went off on a beautiful tangent, but a tangent all the same. Deciding that – since I had the serotonin still flowing for accomplishing a thing on my plastic ball list – I wrote this.

I've taught myself a few ways to organize and help myself. With so many articles available online and so many people willing to share their personal journeys with being neurodivergent, I have learned a few new tips and ideas to help myself function without needing something urgent happening in order to respond.

The same things that make me an excellent candidate for a successful career in Emergency Medical Services, make it harder for me to be productive for myself while being retired after injury and living by myself. The cats NEED to be fed and given clean water. That's easy. I'd never forget to take care of them. So why is it less easy to remember to feed and medicate myself in a timely manner? When living with my family I'd never forget to grocery shop, prepare meals, and clean. Yet for just me, by myself, it never seems worth the effort. It's not depression. It's a lack of productive distraction by means of a call to action. The body at rest will stay at rest.

Since this body at rest has trouble getting motivated into motion, I understand more and more why I can love the *idea* of going to events. I can look forward to events. When it's time to prepare to go to said event, I can't get motivated, organized or moving. Where I used to bully myself, I have learned better ways to motivate myself to do good things and give good experiences to myself. While I still get overwhelmed to the point of not wanting to go and convince myself no one will care if I don't make it, because Emotional Impermanence tells me if I am out of sight, I'm out of mind, I have learned that it is a 'me' issue and because I am just wired differently. I have learned to reach out to others who I have shared excitement over attending the event with and together, ignite a spark of renewed excitement.

I have been shocked to discover that the people I was once intimidated by (not because they were mean or aloof but because they were obviously loved and respected, always surrounded by people who wanted to share time with and talk with them, so obviously they had no time for me) – also felt the way I did.

They had the same trouble accepting what past experience showed them. They were loved and desired among community for more than just what they could do. They were loved for who they are and have always been.

The Rainbow Goddess is here to empower us all. I am coming to believe that we are all on the spectrum, even if only a little bit. I find it empowering to learn about all the different aspects of Neurodivergency. It doesn't make me feel normalized or feel like I have a place to fit it. It just helps to remind me that what I feel and how I think is perfectly normal for me. I don't need to fit in to survive within a neurotypical society. I just need to know how to function in society in a way that empowers me to continue to grow and thrive while still being able to live on my own terms.

I love that the more I learn the easier it has become to help others too. After all, we're all just trying to find our own way home. And for at least a part of the journey, I find it can be so much nicer when we can find ways to walk together and lend support and compassion while we walk each other through the rainbows of life on our way home to our genuine, authentic selves.

PS: I promptly forgot that I wrote both essays and let them sit in draft files on my laptop for over a week. In a convoluted chain of memory triggers, I was reminded of my essays. The calendar reminded me that I'm fast approaching the deadline to submit. Suddenly, empowered by a cup of tea and a boost of adrenaline (courtesy of a deadline), both essays are cleanly edited and ready to email. It really is no wonder why I thrived in a busy 911 career in the streets of NYC. There is always a call to action, a sense of urgency and a duty to respond. Now, I am learning to make myself a high priority and trying to not wait for it to become urgent so that I remember to give myself gentle care.

When the Ungrieved For Past Besieges the Now

Lucy Pierce

A Glorious Catastrophe

Lucy Pierce

I never asked for it,
the box you gave to me at my birth,
the ask that my vast wild eternal nature
should squeeze itself inside
and make a home for itself.
So excruciatingly crippling,
the conditions of my service.
Maybe it never really mattered after all
that I wasn't ever quite lovable enough,
or desirable enough for you.
Not pleasing or pretty enough,
never quite malleable and subservient enough
to win the prize of your gaze.
Maybe I was really just born to be
this glorious catastrophe
of heat and hair
and blood and sweat,
trying to hide itself
from the cruel gaze of the predator,
swirling through time like a force of nature,
untamable, unknowable, unpossessable,
sovereign and free, if only she knew.
Maybe I don't care anymore,
that I don't actually want what you're selling,
that I am not and never was for sale,
that I have nothing to sell that you would want to buy.
Unwanted, unhinged from the world,
an act of revolution,
like a thunderstorm or a wildfire
or a weed that sprouts in the gaps of the pavement.
Because I always was and ever will be
a little piece of everything.
I am birth and death,
and all that comes between,
the amniotic fluid and the first breath,

I am the black shroud and the dark earth,
exquisitely grotesque,
primal and fierce,
delicate and fine.
Maybe I don't even want you to love me any more,
maybe I just want to find the way
to claim a greater playing sphere
than the one you allocated to me.
One that has a place for all the parts of me,
unbound from the contortions of suppression.
If you only knew how big I was,
if only I could let myself truly know that unfathomable fact,
unshackling the edicts of safety you placed on me.
I am not safe,
I am a turbulent channel of rampant love and pain,
a catastrophic deluge of compassionate rage and sensual harbor.
I am unfurling my torrential magnificence
into the co-creative field of the universe,
I am weeping in the darkness of my exile.
I am a grief-stricken burgeoning,
a primal harbor for lost parts
and misplaced dreams,
I am big enough to hold all the brokenness and all the hope,
a majestic annihilation of reason,
a formidable imperative of tenderness.
I do not fit in your box and I have all the scars to prove it.
I will not prune myself for you,
be clipped for your infantilizing whim.
I am hair and juice, snot and tears,
blood and bone, woman born,
all the years my age and powerful,
unkempt and fertile, life-giving warrioress,
bloodcurdling protector of the vulnerable and the weak.
No I am not pretty and I will not be shamed
and as you cast me aside
I feel the primal undercurrents of creation
scoop me up and feed the ancient rivers within,
of this formidable longing to unshackle

Her vibrant potency,
Her ferocious transmutation,
transcending the captivity of feminine identity,
the psychic imprisonment of fear and belittlement,
that a colonizing culture enforced upon Her.
I exalt the mossy crevices you would manicure and poison,
I relish the succulent decay you would sanitize and bleach,
I trust in the blood-swelling, bone-crunching,
nectar-flowing, sweat-drenched
brutality of her primordial love,
so tender and fierce.
I will make of Her my home.
I don't want to please you anymore,
I just want to love myself,
in all my magnificent messiness,
a potent mix of all the things a life can be,
born only this once,
as this particular catastrophe of love and grief,
untamable after all the trying,
only able to be loved completely
by a consciousness as vast and unknowable as its own self.
I can rest there, in that knowing,
that even though the world would not have me as I truly am,
I know that the place from which I came will take me back,
unapologetic and shining.
She will understand that I was just an ugliness
too exquisite for the world of small boxes,
a beauty too primal and pungent,
too real and honest
for the world of masks.

Stage Fright

Barbara O'Meara

Oil on Wood Panel

Nourishing Giftedness:
Neurodiversity and Niche Construction

Stephanie Mines, Ph.D.

WHAT IS *Niche Construction?*

Niche construction is a concept derived from biology in which an organism makes adjustments to its own environment. It is a feedback response system because not only does the organism change but the environment also changes as a product of relational interaction. A clear example is when beavers change their environments by constructing dams or when earthworms change the soil they inhabit. In both cases the result is co-evolutionary. Proximal environmental modifications often spread out further, creating whole system shifts.

If we apply this paradigm to sensory integration and human development, we see that when we create a contained environment of advocacy and individuated attunement the ramifications permeate into the home and family environment alongside the school and therapy environments. The examples in this compilation revolve around constructing a niche or arena in which a child has at close hand and ready access the supportive resources needed to become whole and integrated as he or she is. These resources are tailored to what the individual child needs to express herself optimally without the frustrations of burdensome sensory overload.

How to Nourish Giftedness in Sensory Challenged Youth

"My ideas come in streams and my only difficulty
is to hold them fast."
~Nikola Tesla

Storms of imagination and inspiration, acute sensitivity to all sensory input, driving over-focus and inwardness are all common traits for people with sensory integration imbalances. Some of the most brilliant contributors to human culture and evolution have exhibited aspects of these characteristics. By investigating their lives, we can learn about parenting sensory needs children. In this chapter I convene a conference of models and mentors from biographies that become a cornucopia of limbic nourishment. This gathering identifies the key ingredients for nourishing giftedness in sensory challenged, autistic, and neurodiverse young people. The dominant characteristics we can identify for sensory abundant children include:

1. Heightened powers of observation;
2. Acute sensitivity to stimuli;
3. Receptivity to images and visual thinking;
4. A compelling, complex, unique and rich inner world;
5. Unique insight;
6. Creative and out-of-the box problem solving ideas;
7. Profound determination, sometimes seen as stubbornness;
8. Development that is out-of-sync;
9. Inwardness; and
10. Over-focus on certain chosen subjects, interests and/or activities.

The three key gifts that adults can cultivate, alongside their love for the specialness of their unique child, to nourish giftedness in the children who have these traits are:

1. Differentiating themselves from the children they care for by retracting projection;
2. Advocating for the learning styles that are developmentally appropriate and encouraging for each child; and
3. Finding the therapies and therapists that meet the child where he is for optimum enhancement, growth, and development. See the Resource Annex chapter for samples of how to find these options.

I explore these ten characteristics and the three key gifts of the adults who serve them through the lives of people who have struggled with sensory integration and made their contributions, nevertheless. Their self-reported life experiences allow us to see what works and what doesn't work to enhance and stabilize the rare brilliance of our sensory needs children and youth.

**The Recipe for Supporting Differentiation:
Theory of Mind + Empathy**

Adults have a lot to learn from the lives of sensory-challenged children and youth. One of the characteristics of sensory abundance is heightened self-awareness. I have frequently been astounded by how my sensory-challenged and autistic patients reveal incredible insight into themselves and others. What they lack is perspective. Because adults have the cognitive capacity to find perspective and to reflect on their own development, they can create a theory of mind if they cultivate profound self-awareness.

Once adults create a theory of mind for themselves then it is possible for them to cultivate a theory of mind for the children in their care.

Theory of mind, differentiation and empathy are like the Three Muses for those who serve children with sensory overload. Theory of mind means that you have a developmental perspective and can temper your language, presence, educational and therapeutic interventions to meet that perspective for each child. You can, for instance, understand an autistic child in the context not only of their neurology but also their home life and the parenting they receive.

When I was conducting my recent clinical trials, I encountered many autistic children whose parents were veterans of combat. The relationship between Post-Traumatic Stress Disorder (PTSD), autism and the neurochemistry of fear has yet to be fully explored but it was evident in the lives of these children. The Autism National Committee notes that despite fairly abundant anecdotal evidence, knowledge of the nature, prevalence, and treatment of psychological trauma in the lives of neurodiverse people is lacking. (Autism National Committee 2007) For these autistic sons and daughters of veterans the presence of PTSD in their home environment was a significant component in the theory of mind I cultivated for them.

Differentiation requires self-awareness and self-understanding. Adults need to bear witness to how they respond to children. If, for instance, you are threatened by the way in which your child stands out or does not fit in then it is up to you to explore what that means about you. Trace this reaction to its source and take responsibility for it so that you do not project your fears, shame, need to deny, suppress, blame, or compensate onto a child. Anything that prevents you from seeing a child's experience from their perspective requires investigation.

Divine Girl Child

Arna Baartz

Closing The Gap

Lucy Pierce

Closing the gap,
between love and fear,
between exile and belonging,
between mind and earth,
between pain and care.
So that we are all wet and sleek as newborns,
brushed with the dust of earth,
gathered into arms of kindness,
coming home,
return
return,
return.
No space for shame or judgement,
just communion and attunement,
to the finest ripple of need.

Closing the gap
between shame and unified nurturance,
between trauma and embodied integration,
between blame and rightful atonement.
So that body and skin,
feeling and thought,
inner and outer,
become lovers,
pressed tight in reconciliation,
so that psyche returns to the birthright of earth,
to the embrace of kindness and kin,
returns to primal unity,
to sovereign power,
returns,
returns,
returns.

Closing the gap
between thought and action,
between bigotry and restitution,
between prejudice and restoration,
between abuse and safety,
between isolation and inclusivity,
between manipulation and regeneration.
So that only love remains,
fierce and brave,
in all Her wild faces.
And deep listening also
at the interface of self and other and the in-between,
eternal homecoming,
genesis,
return,
return.

Closing the gap
between the spite of domination and benevolent sovereignty,
between history and the healing presence to love's living moment,
between agony and nourishment,
between the orphaned and the inclusive hearth.

Closing the gap
between belief and action,
between injustice and attuned advocacy,
between the injury of betrayal
and fiercely accountable acknowledgment,
Closing the gap so that we all become kin
at the feasting place of creation.
To each partake of the pristine succour
of our empowered existence
inside an ecologically embedded macrocosm of grace.
No longer split and splintered
and brutal and cruel,
but returned,
returned,
returned.

Closing the gap
between the unfathomable grief and an embodied shore,
between violent rage and rightful justice,
between dissociated terror and deeply courageous feeling,
between brutal incarceration and regenerative healing,
between shackled suppression and exuberant expression,
between need and privilege,
between brutal travesty and artful remedy.
So that body and skin and world and self
and human and land and cosmos
and animal and plant and microbiome
and fire and water and earth and air
and spirit
sit together at the one fire,
in reciprocal alignment,
coexistent in a unified field of belonging
and love,
tender and fierce,
in all Her wild faces.

Closing the gap
between dream and lived immersion,
between prayer and reality,
between hope and accountable becoming.
So that the wound that will not heal,
the shame scar as deep as Hades,
will always be given wing and balm,
the smoke of prayers,
the touch of care,
and succour and vision,
and a friendly hand to hold in the dark times.
So that we may each walk at peace
with our very own deaths,
life-giving,
so that we are made rich again
and whole and kind and brave.

Closing the gap within.
Closing the gap without.
Return.
Return.
Return,
to love
in all Her fierce
and wild
and tender
faces.

Belonging

Lucy Pierce

147

Discovering My Personal Neurodiversity

Stephanie Mines, PhD

When I wrote *New Frontiers in Sensory Integration* in 2014, my aim was to serve the families I was supporting with neurodiverse children. These young people were adopted, had been conceived in an IVF or surrogacy situation, were on the autistic spectrum, had eating disorders, structural struggles, or the children had behavioral problems and health issues that included sensory difficulties. There were also children with combinations of these issues.

To meet the needs of these families and their precious, brilliant children I did a significant amount of research. This led to clinical trials that I conducted over a three-year period. I interviewed Occupational and Physical Therapists and worked side-by-side with them in clinics.

I always enjoyed working with these families, and found the children to be consistently intelligent, engaged, responsive and delightful. Eventually I conducted family clinics in my office, bringing in various specialists to work with me. We thoroughly documented everything we did and followed the families for as long as we could. My clinical, peer reviewed research showed that in small, pilot projects, the interventions that I offered, including subtle applied touch, were successful in producing significant shifts for children. A statistical analysis of a pilot project with autistic children ages 5-11 years showed remarkable improvement in daily life skills and learning. That analysis is available in the published articles.

Neurodiverse Children Mirror My Own Neurodiversity

What surprised me the most in all of this was the uncovering of my own neurodiversity. Coming from a family without attunement, attachment or bonding instincts or skills, nor the capacity to access appropriate resources, none of my developmental needs were recognized. In retrospect, looking at my own evolution through the mother and grandmother eyes that I now have, I see that I was an acutely sensitive child (for which I was severely criticized and reprimanded), with powerful perceptions, verging on the mystical, and an amazing capacity for empathy. This empathy became the adaptation skill that allowed me to survive. I used it to stay out of trouble as much as possible and to be of service to my family members. Of course, my defiance would erupt periodically, but I did my best to keep it in check. This was horrific for me personally. It distorted my intelligence. It fragmented me so severely that I am still not fully reassembled back into my Original Brilliance. Original Brilliance is the term I have created to reflect unique, innate creativity.

Contrary to the highly touted and oft-quoted research of Dr. Simon Baron-Cohen, who graduate students in neuroscience put on a pedestal, I never saw children diagnosed with autism as averse to touch and eye-contact. All the children I met, on the contrary, were receptive to connection and, if anything, aware of and responsive to everything around them. However, when they sensed that others were not respectful of them or paying attention, those children would sometimes, if not often, withdraw. I believe I was also this kind of child. My mother describes me as very quiet and subdued. Anyone who knows me now would not use those adjectives for me.

The children who I served as a clinician were the ones who taught me about my own neurodiversity. Recently, when I was reviewing my early writing from my adolescence and young adulthood, I saw that I was recording profound perceptions about the world around me, and especially the adults in my environment. I was also extremely sensitive to what I can only describe as vibratory fields from the natural world. I kept all this hidden as I knew that sharing these experiences was risky because everything about revealing myself to my family was risky, sometimes even life-threatening.

I was fortunate, I suppose, that I was so good at adapting to these circumstances. This did require squelching outward signs of intense creativity. I was made to feel ashamed for my uniqueness, even ridiculed, so I stopped revealing it. That is adaptation. The truth is, though, that such masking never worked. My creativity was irrepressible, and therefore I felt trapped in my longing to be loved and seeing the only option for that as being someone I could not become.

What I am is a unique human being with a powerful contribution to make. This is true of everyone. Because this was never mirrored back to me, I have been required to spend most of my life discovering it. Every child should know she is gifted. The greatest struggle in my life is believing in myself. I think this struggle is responsible for most of my suffering.

The Rise of Neurodiverse Intelligence in the Midst of Climate Crisis

It is the electrifying alacrity of my neurodiverse creativity that frequently stuns and disarms others. Yet it is perfectly suited to this time of climate crisis. My creativity has a suction-like focusing force. Like a high-powered vacuum cleaner, it won't let go. My brand of neurodiversity charts unmapped territories with poems and theories articulated in language that makes people gasp, often in disbelief. I use words that are familiar, but they render novel experiences and link what was unknown to what can be known.

For my neurodiverse mind, overload or overwhelm is familiar. It is not to be eschewed. On the contrary, it is the stuff of life. My sensory filters were broken long before I was born. They have reconfigured themselves in unpredictable, improvisatory ways. My neurodiverse intelligence is sand painting after sand painting, so elusive sometimes that I miss it myself.

I have developed a neural net that catches the confetti of my perceptions and contains it for the purpose of serving others and making poetry and whatever other writing comes through my hands onto the page. I distill sensory input in a way that is ineffable, even to me. I am also a metallurgist. My particular jewels are made from a magnitude of grief that has no etiology I can articulate or any destination that I know. It is timeless.

My fast-acting, quick-to-rise neurodiversity moves always in the direction of manifestation. Manifestation is a physiological urge and a troublemaker, as it requires support that I frequently do not have. I have to fast track, almost all the time, because of this. I am a juggler of necessity. I would prefer a more spacious lifestyle. Finding the support systems, the wherewithal, including the finances, to keep pace with my lightning bolt creativity is quite challenging. It is likely also grounding as it makes me confront the nitty-gritty, day-to-day, and stay in place when I would much prefer to fly away.

Honoring Uniqueness: The Power of Self-Respect

If I could offer only one suggestion to parents it is to model self-respect, especially for neurodiverse children who are often publicly ridiculed. Self-respect is named here not for achievements at all, but for uniqueness of being. The consequences of not being introduced to the potency of self-respect are quite severe, in my experience. I need to reconstruct self-respect every day. Thankfully I now succeed more often than I fail. Sometimes it takes me hours, even days. But self-respect is the light at the end of the tunnel. It is an end in itself. It is the key to satisfaction and peace.

With all the talk about the Polyvagal System, healing the inner child, stress-relief, Internal Family Systems, and mindfulness, I would say the key to all of the above is self-respect for Original Brilliance, as I have defined it here. In a climate changing world, one might wonder at the activism of promoting self-respect for Original Brilliance. Yet I see it as one of the central pieces of puzzle of creating a groundswell tipping point to turn our suicidal, self-sabotaging actions around.

Women and Neurodiversity

The patriarchal colonization of the feminine, in which all women marinate, beginning even before conception, gives rise to compensatory strategies that weave with the particular traumatic and shocking circumstances of individual families and cultures. These compensatory strategies can be symptomatically classified as aspects of neurodiversity, and sometimes illnesses, even structural distortions. We women will bend and shape ourselves in all sorts of ways to be of service, to survive, and to deliver our messages. This is particularly true when empathy without sensory filtering or boundaries is a driving force, uniting us so intimately with the needs of others that we become indistinguishable from them. In short bursts, or transient interludes, this sometimes wins us the love we want. It does not, however, have endurance, so we are left scurrying for more and more compensations. That insane pattern ends with authentic self-respect for Original Brilliance.

The distortion of the feminine, taking the form sometimes of neurodiversity for which we, as women, feel responsible as if it were an error on our part, is coming to an end. Neurodiversity is indeed a skill set in these times of unprecedented escalation and dissolution. Our personal struggles in the direction of self-respect deserve enormous support. I am dedicated to providing that, including by freeing myself of my own self-harming thoughts and liberating self-respect for myself into a way of life. Please join me, my dear sisters, in this crusade. Our time is now to rise beyond trauma into wholeness, in service to the true Mother who has always nurtured us.

Copyright April 2022

Soulskin

Lucy Pierce

Both/And

Molly Remer

"I wish I could say what I really mean and be heard,"
I wrote these words
when I was a tired and tender new mother
less than three months postpartum
aching for who I used to be,
struggling to integrate this new self,
immersed in the forged fires
of early motherhood,
longing for the strong hand of love in mine
and starving for myself.
Sometimes I still feel this sensation,
that I wish I could fully express how I feel:
thready and worn,
ragged and alone,
gasping and breathless,
awash with anxiety and panting
before the mountain,
while also expressing
how I am simultaneously
alive with purpose,
blazing with ideas and power,
burning with enthusiasm,
flushed with passion.
How I am sometimes
stunned by my own brilliance
and often humbled
by my own weariness
and the sensation I've created
something too big for me to hold
while simultaneously wanting to do

Even.
More.
I'm allowed to be frazzled and flourishing,
worn and wondrous.
It is astounding to witness
how I am charred and I am glowing,
I am inspired and I am parched.
I wish I could state these two realities out loud:
the shining brilliance
and the ragged fatigue
and simply have them both held,
with no one fixing me
and without fixing myself,
without assuming there is anything to change,
without assuming
or implying that anything is wrong,
but simply acknowledging that this is here
in my cupped hands:
one full of blazing light,
the other filled with the only shreds I have left
and they are so small.
Perhaps I can bring them both together
in front of my heart,
press them under my bones
into my flesh,
and know that it is possible to be
Both.
And. More.
Much.
and All,
rolled together
into a sometimes unbearable,
sometimes blazing
bundle of fire, ash, and skin.

Recipe To My Mess

Jessica Huff

About this piece:

"Recipe to my mess" is part of an Illustrated journaling project that I have been working on over the past year and is inspired by some of the challenges I face in my life and at work being neurodivergent. In this piece I share some of the small things that I strive to do in my daily routine that improve my overall quality of life. I hope that this piece can help others and combat the stigma that still exists around the topics of neurodiversity and mental health.

COVID-19 and the Aspie Mind
(Or Is It the Other Way Round?)

Holin Kennen

I have Asperger's Syndrome. There. I said it. Right in front of everyone at work who is reading this right now.

It's huge to say that I am an "Aspie." Terrifying, in fact. The students who shot up Columbine High School were both labeled as Asperger's kids, though I never saw anything definitive on it. Ditto the shooters at Sandy Hook Elementary School and Stoneman Douglas High School. Without any evidence whatsoever, Asperger's Syndrome and "murderer" have become inextricably linked in the American psyche. It's a problem.

To tell someone I have Asperger's is to potentially change a relationship – any relationship – forever, and not always in a positive way. Greta Thunberg, who, at only 16 years old, addressed the UN on climate change in a fiery speech in September 2019 and was *Time Magazine's* Person of the Year, says Asperger's is her "superpower," yet she was vilified by Fox News as a "mentally ill Swedish child" and mocked by no less a personage than the former President of the United States. Twice.

Shortly before I joined this office, I worked in a small law practice. At that small, intimate law office, I was told by the managing partner, "Not everybody would hire someone like you." What did she mean? Someone short? Someone with brown eyes? A woman over 40? Oh, I see. Someone with Asperger's. So, I don't talk about it much.

Aspies as a group are an amazingly intelligent bunch. We know what we know, and we know it well. Ask me about Italian and English history prior to 1650, pre-industrial European technology, sheep and wool, spinning wheels, and chickens, and I can give you more information on them than you thought existed. If I don't know the answer to something, I'll dig it up, no matter how obscure the question, and hand it to you as a gift. Aspies are deep thinkers. We go down rabbit holes. Sometimes it takes a while to come out.

Aspies think differently than other people because we are different. Many of us can relate to Spock and his feelings of alienation from the rest of the Enterprise crew: His sense of logic in the face of puzzling human passions. It wasn't that he didn't have emotions; he just dealt with them differently. Aspies tend to have anxiety because we want to fit in with everybody else, but like Spock, we can't figure out how. It's awkward.

Aspies tend to think outside the box – way outside the box – which is our superpower. In fact, we live outside of the box most of the time. The thing is, we need a box to think out of. Boxes help us know where we are and what to do. Simple things like trying to figure out where I put my toothbrush in a hotel bathroom are humorous, but they're a real thing. Not having tea in the morning is cause for stress in my life. When I have order in my daily life, I can stretch out beyond the box and get creative. I don't want to be stuck in the box; I just need edges to hold on to. When I have those, I can do amazing things.

COVID-19 has taken away my boxes. It has crushed them, burnt them, and thrown them in the bin. Nothing is predictable; I can't plan for contingencies. I can't just "be in the moment" because the moment is a moving target, and I need it to stay still long enough to analyze. Yes, I love working from home, with my nice window that looks out on the trees and lawns of my town, but it's also disorienting to work here. Home and work are supposed to occur in separate places. They don't mix. Ever. (I've been known not to recognize colleagues from work if I see them on the street.) In the face of COVID chaos, my Aspie mind goes something like this: Shouldn't we be making a plan? Somebody is supposed to know what to do here, right? Because I sure don't. Why are the people who seem to know what's going on being ignored by the people in charge? What do I need to do instead on Thursday nights when my knitting group should be meeting at my house? It makes no sense, and sense is what is important to an Aspie. There has to be a box out there somewhere.

So, I'm trying to use my own superpowers in this unpredictable time to see all of this through the lens of history and to reduce the anxiety that comes with uncertainty. How have people dealt with plagues in the past? What did we do to survive and to help each other? How did we make art and expand civilization in the midst of chaos? What do I know how to help in the present? Someone has thought outside the box. Someone must have found a box. I'll keep looking for it.

Some people with Asperger's have found therapy helpful. I have too, on occasion, but it's limited. It doesn't change who I am. You can't "fix" Asperger's. It just is. But perhaps there's a new paradigm that will emerge from these events where people hold close to the things that really matter – each other – and freely toss away all the rest. Where people like me are seen as a resource for creative thinking and problem solving, especially in times of crisis when boxes need to be put aside for a while but still visible. I hope that a "brave new world" is out there somewhere in its own special box. It might be a place where we can all think outside the box to see what's on the other side. That would only be logical.

(Note: This article was written in May 2020 during the isolation of COVID lockdown as part of a series of personal submissions for Mental Health Awareness month in my employer's international online newsletter. I almost didn't write it. Many people with Asperger's Syndrome have different experiences than mine, but I tried to write about my own experience and those of people with Asperger's, particularly women, that I have personally known.)

Harmony

Kat Shaw

Hail and Welcome to the Rainbow Chakra Balancing Goddess.
Send your colourful cleansing love into every energy point of my
body and soul so that I may come into Divine alignment and
realise my true potential and gloriousness.
Fill me with your hues so that I walk like a Goddess
beside you in harmony.

Tigers Dancing: A Contemplation for Those who Experience Neurodiversities

Katie Bee

Have you ever wondered what your diagnosis/es might be if you were free to diagnose yourself? How you might language yourself? Many of us will have been diagnosed, named, labelled by, if you're like me, any number of different health practitioners: GPs, Psychiatrists, Therapists (Freudian and Jungian) Nurses, Healers, Shamans, Coaches, Spiritual Teachers and more... But have you ever wanted, do you want, could you want, to name your own 'condition?' To find your own expression of your individual experience? Instead of receiving a 'diagnosis?' And how different that might feel? I have.

For me, diagnosis is a double-edged sword. Diagnoses hold comfort and terror. The comfort is in knowing I am not alone – I am a member of a community, a tribe. There are others like me. As 'neurodiverse' I know I am not singular, I am one of many, we are Rainbow. To almost-quote Whitman, we "contain multitudes." This is also the beauty of 'neurodiversity' as a 'diagnosis' – it's a newer, kinder, and more attuned way to language many people's experiences. So, a huge upside of diagnosis is a sense of community, if you're lucky enough to find one, or perhaps, be allocated one via available (if available!) health care/therapeutic services.

The downside, the terror, is stigma. The tragedy of stigma offers the opposite of community, brings a hiding, a living-in-shame-and-fear, closeted, afraid to be close to others, afraid of being 'found out,' afraid 'to tell.' I am afraid to tell, have for years and years been afraid 'to tell,' and yet here, now, for you and for girl gods and neurodiverse women everywhere, I am stepping up. I am writing this for you in an attempt to 'come out' of my stigma-closet, and re-naming, re-imagining, re-languaging my diagnosis is integral to that. Hello! I'm Katie Bee.

So. In wondering what it might be like to describe and language my own interior experience I have imagined a conversation that instead of answering the question "What's wrong with me?" goes something like this:

You: What's happening? Can you name or describe your experience? What are things like for you now? What would you like to be called?

Me: I see tigers. It feels a bit like wrestling, snarling, tigers.

You: That sounds intense. And a bit scary.

Me: Yes, it's really intense. And sometimes very scary.

But that's not all there is. There's a beach, at night, and the full moon. That's when they dance.

So, I feel something like "Tigers dancing on the seashore under a full moon."

You: Intense! Painfully beautiful.

Me: Yes. Painfully beautiful.

And sometimes the sea is wild, wild as anything! Stormy! Terribly stormy! Wild seas, wrestling-dancing tigers, full moon, wind.

***

Of course, it's not always like this. Deep Depression has a different tone. Darker colours. A flatter landscape, sometimes almost like "Nothing-At-All."

You: Where are you now? How would you describe it?

Me: It's a cloak. No, not a cloak. A shroud. A clingy, sticky shroud. Bottom of a hill. No, a mountain. A mountain made of treacle sponge and tar. Climbing a heavy treacle mountain wading through tar wearing a shroud. With no eye holes.

You: Hard work!

Me: Bloody hard work! And sometimes, nothing. And always, no-one. Can't move. Just darkness. Cool. Empty. Raw. Alone.

This is called "Bleak."

This is called "Empty Dark Day."

This is called "The Song of Sorrows."

***

And – it's not always like that. Our experience shifts, moves, changes. We all know the old chestnut: "This, too, shall pass." So sometimes there's vibrancy! And let's not forget joy! I personally believe the 'HSP' and SPS aspects of my neurodiversity bring me a deeper appreciation of joy and wonder, trigger spiritual realizations, and offer a deep attunement to 'Source,' to Goodness, to the Goddess. They offer Communion.

You: What's that like? Who are you now?

Me: I am shimmering light. I am iridescence. I am acutely sensitive.

I feel every tremor, every sound, and am all of it.

I feel the rustle of leaves, the footfall of mice, the breathing of birds.

I am called "Trembling Aspen."

I have no skin. I am space, I feel the beating of your heart, my heart.

I am called "Everything."

I am called "Goddess."

I am called "Rainbow."

I am called "Love."

***

In *Belonging Here – A Guide for the Spiritually Sensitive Person*, therapist and spiritual teacher Judith Blackstone describes five paradigms of "spiritual sensitivity" all of which I would personally equate with some aspect of 'neurodiversity.' Her work has been profoundly helpful to me, once more in knowing 'not-aloneness,' in performing the work of de-stigmatization, and in the offering of comfort, inspiration, healing, and support. Her work has offered me hope in many very dark times and I encourage all of you who haven't come across it to check it out! Blackstone writes that her hope is that her work helps the 'Spiritually Sensitive Person' (her term) "feel more accepting and appreciative of your sensitivity, your emotional depth, and your big mind. Each of these gifts is an entranceway into your true nature, which is more miraculous than anything we can imagine." Understanding and coming to know this is also part of my own journey with neurodiversity. The truth outlined here is that neurodiversity, in the form of spiritual sensitivity, is a gift from the gods.

Speaking of whom – in Greek mythology the Goddess of the Rainbow is Iris, and in some texts, it is Iris, not Hermes, who is their messenger. Travelling on the wind and on her rainbows, she delivers messages between mortals and Olympians. She is also tasked with offering the Pantheon nectar to drink to refresh and nurture them. Likewise, she offers us succour. Iris, Rainbow Goddess, is sometimes golden-winged and at other times takes the form of the Rainbow itself, and the Rainbow is a paradigm which suits neurodiversity very well. All colours of the spectrum are here, are necessary, and are welcome. Iris's very being is diversity. The gods and goddesses themselves spell diversity, and diversity is good – it's essential, we need diversity just as, as a species, we need, have needed, sensitivity.

This is something made explicit in Elaine Aron's articulation of the 'Highly Sensitive Person,' where, historically, she explains, heightened sensitivity determined our survival. For instance, a more sensitive, alert member of a group of preyed-upon, hunted animals (such as antelopes) would alert the tribe to the approach of predators (such a lions) thus ensuring the survival of as many of the tribe as possible. Clearly, survival itself has, since ancient times, been one of the gifts of increased (atypical) sensitivity, which, for me goes hand-in-hand with what I would call my neurodiversity. (And I can only speak for me.)

Without doubt however, the greatest gift I've been offered by neurodiversity is 'Great Compassion.' Compassion and care for others and, in particular for others who are experiencing states of acute aloneness and suffering similar to my own. I have gifts of deep empathy, deep care, deep concern. A big ole wide-open, broken, acutely sensitive and ever-loving heart. Thus, for me, Guan Yin with her thousand arms as well as Iris, the Rainbow Goddess, is an archetype for neurodiversity. And so, I also have other names:

"Broken-Open Heart."

"All-Embracing Mother."

"Ancient Oak Tree in Open Field, Waving at Birds."

Returning then full circle to my initial question of naming ourselves, naming our experiences, in our own way, with our own imaginations: How might it be if we gave ourselves our own names? Who would we be? If given the freedom to translate our own feelings and interior experiences, into language? Who would you be? And how might this change how you feel?

Mostly I am "Tigers Dancing,
            Beside Stormy Seas
            Under a Full Moon."

And I am brave.

Who are you, when you are free to choose your name?

Speak to Yourself Kindly

Arna Baartz

My Rainbow Brain

Wakanda Rose

A car crash. One split second of a moment was all that it took to change my entire life. I had always been different and what is seen as neurodivergent, yet the car crash I was in really brought alive the full capacity of my rainbow brain.

As I write this, it's been nearly 3 years since my dad and I were rear ended at 70mph and I can confidently say I'm landing in a place of deep acceptance of my brain and being. That was not always the case, absolutely not.

I'm reminded of a time I was younger where I was fully in my own power and in my full creative mode, then I realised not many people were like me. I soon started observing other people's behaviour to learn how to fit in and be more like them so I would be more accepted. I lost me in the process. I was existing in the role of people pleaser and having shallow connections with people around me. When I did be me in front of others I was called "weird", asked if I had ADHD or Autism...a lot, so 16-year-old me went back into being someone she was not. It was a painful existence that led to a lot of self-abusive behaviours.

I always had 2 strong parts to my inner world for as long as I can remember. One deeply strong in her no, could see and feel everyone's shadow selves, accepted death was a reality from such a young age yet terrified by it, was full of anger towards people who hurt other beings and fear was also a strong shadow that followed me for as long as I can recall. The other part of me was deeply in love with life, saw the best in everybody, empathized with anyone and everything and deeply accepted people. These parts clashed, always.

When I explored the Norse Freyja Priestess Path, I felt a strong connection to Hel and Freyja Vanadis. These archetypes felt like they represented these 2 strong parts to me. As I have followed and committed deeper with the Goddess Path, I found a deeper allowing to take a deep breathe into myself and love these 2 strong parts of my inner world more. The more I explore the Goddess path, the more I accept myself, seeing myself in Freyja and Kali.

Something changed when I was 22. This big moment of enough came alive in me and using my beautiful rainbow brain I found a creative solution out of the inner turmoil. I was to go to India. By no means did India cure anything – it actually put me face-to-face with my shadows in a foreign land. I decided I would be fully me here since I didn't know these people, nor would I ever have to see them again.

India was the planting of a seed. Like any journey of a seed, it comes with being plunged into the dark and unknown. Cracking out of the shell is no easy job nor is it for the faint hearted. I feel the path to the Goddess is not all love and light and ascending into the clouds, no, it thrusts you into the deep dark where all beautiful things go to grow. Just like the flowers, the plants, and the herbs, we must return to the Goddess to truly become.

When I came back from India, there was this push pull happening inside of me. The old, programmed people pleaser me and the new fuck-it-I'm-me part. I slowly found the old me was running the show again and depression came back in full force.

The Goddess has a way of bringing you back to her no matter how far you stray from the path. The car accident I was in was that moment that cemented my relationship with the Goddess. There's no cure for my neurodivergent brain. Following the Goddess path has led me to deep acceptance of this and enhanced my own inner world to be able to hold all parts of me. The anger and fear that once was at the driving seat of my reality

– and my mind doing all I could to suppress these parts – are now welcomed as sacred parts of me. The Goddess path has allowed me to fully open and blossom with no shame towards myself. Basking in the arms of the Goddess has allowed me to grow tools that self-soothe and self-regulate me, for the power has always been deep within me. "For why does the Serpent eat herself, because everything she seeks is within".

I drum for myself every day. I rattle to myself to soothe myself. I walk bare foot most places. I allow myself to have a toddler tantrum for those moments emotions feel too much. I allow myself to get excited at the smallest of things. I do all I need to for me regardless of current societal constructs. My rainbow brain and way of being deserves a place in the light now.

I've learnt that as big as my trauma and pain vortex are, they are as immense as my healing vortex is. And by damn, it's a big ass vortex … Rightfully so – I deserve to be me. We all deserve to be our true selves.

There's a collateral beauty in seeing the world in a Rainbow Brain way. Following the Goddess path felt like a homecoming, allowing myself to land into my Rainbow Brain rather than contort myself into someone I am not. I. am. Home.

Firecracker

Kat Shaw

I am Firecracker. Hear me roar.
Feisty. Fierce. Alive.
I bow to nobody.
Know your power.

Neurodiversity Holds Keys to Unlock Patriarchal Prisons

Trinity Shea Thomas

Great news! Neurodiversity (ND) holds keys to unlock patriarchal prisons. What has been used against us can be turned inside out to set us free.

ND codes safely unzipping in our neurology escort us from apologies to superpowers.

The challenge for me in writing about this was to talk myself off the ledge of entirely earned outrage and stay firmly in the increasingly familiar realm of celebration, where all the many Truths retain their capitals and we are securely positioned to win the race of human. I will be taking full advantage of neurodivergent license, a step or twirl beyond poetic license.

I didn't have a word for how I am designed for a long time. I knew I was different, definitely one of those who was not like the others. I lived my life as an apology.

The word neurodiversity was created in 1996 to describe diagnosed deficits in learning and thinking processes on the autism spectrum. I prefer Harvard Health's recent definition:

> "Neurodiversity describes the idea that people experience and interact with the world around them in many different ways; there is no one 'right' way…"

This 'no one right way' business is the patriarchy's worst nightmare, as it should be. The neurodiverse are uncontrollable by design. It's our superpower. But I'm getting a bit ahead of my tale.

My Own Neurodiverse Design

My brand of neurodiversity is the extra-sensory sort. I was born with enhanced senses, as if I had less filters or had a blowhole open in the top of my head that let more in. I saw, heard, felt, and knew things that no one around me could verify. And these abnormal sensings were the favorite parts of my life. I found real companionship and truth there. I still do.

Tragedy struck when I realized I could not share them. This confused me! Why would I see, hear, feel, and know all of these marvelous things if they were not to be shared with my family and friends? Was I just simply flawed? 'Twas a mystery that required discovery.

I was convinced, over the first dozen years of my life, to keep quiet about everything outside the reality most people lived in. I apologized continuously for all that I saw, heard, felt, and knew. For all that I was. I was shamed into silence.

My life became about exploring how to move from shrinking from my differences to putting them to work in service. I began to look for the others who did not fit in. I found that my ND, before I ever heard the word, was neither a deficit nor a *disorder*, but rather a power of a *higher* order. Occasionally it even saved a life.

Eventually, I stopped hiding and apologizing and got to work. Now I know there are many of us. And we hold crucial keys.

I must admit I was relieved when Malcolm Gladwell published his book, "Blink," in 2007 about how we often 'know without knowing.' He provided a case study of an expensive museum statue that turned out to be fake. The many experts hired to assess it did not agree about whether it was or was not. The ones who 'knew' it was fake could not say how they knew. They just did. And they were correct! *My people!*

Extreme sensitivities often accompany our higher order powers. As a child it was nearly impossible, for example, for me to cut roses for the dinner table. I heard their cries. No one could convince me it didn't hurt them.

I learned to mask my reactions to pass for normal. Usually. Particularly in women, masking leads to a loss of sense, of self, with an increased vulnerability to patriarchal control. We accept the stigma and gaslight ourselves, incrementally dismantling our truth in exchange for acceptance, sanctuary, and belonging. It's a survival strategy and a recoverable error.

As my accumulated life experience and research yielded success, I felt most at home in the arms of nature and the rainbow goddess, the self-sustaining natural wells of love and truth.

When I found myself at my wit's end, I would wrap myself around a tree until I was better. *It always works.*

I found myself regularly at odds with the dominant paradigm. One of its names is Patriarchy.

Patriarchal Prisons – Misogyny and Anecdotal Evidence

I don't have enough pages to catalogue the abuses of the patriarchal system. And I'm committed to staying out of the Outrage Zone. I'm focusing on my top two.

Misogyny and the invalidation of individual truth are patriarchal plot lines designed to enforce powerful prisons. They target agency.

A famous example of this was the women who knew too much and bowed too little – being burned as witches, among other things. And even more astonishing, a successful campaign through *history* to make us fear the witches rather than their murderers.

This became a tried-and-true **Formula**:

> **Step One:** Label something to create fear or discredit it.
> **Step Two:** Ostracize or destroy it.
> **Step Three:** Absolve or even glorify the perpetrators.

Misogyny

The assault on the feminine, misogyny, is not new. It's thousands of years overdue for a rewrite.

Ironically, ancient patriarchal cultures conspired to deprive women, the natural heiresses to goddess culture, of the right to any religious leadership. The Council of Nicea, a Council of Christian Bishops in Turkey in 325 AD, removed women from the priesthood despite women being equally honored as the original apostles of Christ. In about 400 AD, the Oracles of Delphi closed their well of inspiration and walked away after more than a thousand years when the Priests of Apollo began telling them what to say based on who would pay the most to fill their coffers.

Until recently, the patriarchy successfully conspired to deny woman all sorts of everyday rights. Women were not allowed to own property, including themselves, or have the right to vote as a citizen. Even now there are gaps in the right to financial benefits equal to men, including equal pay. And even the right to be sovereign over their own bodies, which is a virulent dispute in my country on this very day.

Why did the patriarchy go to war with women?

They fear our authority and our voices.

Because human life is born through us, exclusively. Because the Rainbow Goddess lives in us. Because a woman's corpus callosum, the bridge between the sides of the brain, contains more nerve fibers than a male's. This gives us greater access to the quantum right brain where we are fully present in the moment and know oneness; where the only real authority lives.

Our voices confront their artificial power. And the jig, as they say, is up.

Women are less often diagnosed with neurodiversity, often being in their 20's or 30's before they receive a diagnosis, which can be confusing and affect their sense of self. It is generally believed that this is because women naturally mask more to accommodate misogyny.

Neurodiverse women are an even greater thorn in the side of the patriarchy, for we are wired with enhanced senses and knowing, aware of the 'powers' that have our backs, and therefore less controllable. *Becoming more so.*

The Rainbow Goddess is rising, in all genders. I can see her smiling as she balances scales.

Anecdotal Evidence

Unlike misogyny, the patriarchy doesn't play gender favorites with dispensing invalidation of lived experience and personal knowing.

Anecdotal evidence is defined as "a factual claim relying only on personal observation and experience, generally regarded as limited in value. It must be backed up by statistical evidence to be accepted as valid." It is considered unreliable. 'Only' anecdotal. And the patriarchy is left securely in charge of reality.

As a practical matter, 'anecdotal evidence' actually means 'your inner knowing and lived experiences just don't count unless we say so.' Dismissive rhetoric delivered with a side of invalidation. It can make us question ourselves. *The worst.*

The assignment of truth and reliability is reserved for governments, corporate boards and research facilities run primarily by an older generation of white men who are taught to value results that are duplicatable and therefore profitable. This is a patriarchal control and profit-based perspective, not a value or truth or solution-driven perspective.

The invalidation of anecdotal evidence is a core strategy of the patriarchy's abuse of power. It's the systemic translation of "You don't know. In fact, you can't know. But we do. *And we will let you know!"*

This scourge has infiltrated nearly every nuance of our society. I am amazed by the reliance on statistics. When I took college courses in statistics, and later used them in corporate settings, the running joke was, "You know, you can prove *anything* with statistics!" And so, they do.

It is past time to create our own statistics of the senses.

In Summary

We have been gaslighted and stigmatized. If we were the fairy Tinkerbell in the book "Peter Pan" by J.M. Barrie, our lights would be dim because we don't believe in ourselves.

Only we can allow our lights to dim! No more apologies!

The real Truth is, there are many Truths, all with their capitals intact. Lived, embodied, personal experience meets a higher standard. It's part of Higher Order Thinking that allows us to synthesize differently to create new facts and new realities. It's a superpower. Rising ND is the antidote for the plague of anecdotal evidence.

Because our senses are different, we open new doors.

Keeping it Real

I'm not advocating that we demonize and discard all patriarchal qualities or accept all anecdotal evidence without vetting it within our own experience and communities. But we mustn't mistake control over nature and other humans as any sort of real power. It's only egoic manipulation and leads to disharmonies and drama. Our world needs *real* power to navigate these changing times. We need a new Call to Arms, not to weaponize our world, but to hold ourselves and each other in loving acceptance.

Real power comes from within and is collaborative. It's matriarchal. And *neurodiverse.*

The Koan of Neurodiversity: Agency and Alchemy

Neurodiversity is a living, embodied koan, the Buddhist's classic paradoxical anecdote or riddle, used in Zen Buddhism to demonstrate the inadequacy of logical reasoning and to provoke enlightenment.

Logic is definitely not invited to this party. Provocation is in play. I can hear Enlightenments cackling in glee around the corner. Patriarchal prisons are predicated on control with its hallmarks of domination, jurisdiction, and management. Neurodiversity establishes a control-free zone. Even in the areas deemed deficit, the neurodiverse are shielded from cultural conditioning as they fail to meet expectations. This is the box-free land of the neurodiverse! The Get Out of Jail Free Zone.

It's past time for Jailbreak. We will use what we *are*, neurodiverse, to unlock patriarchal prisons.

Restoring Agency

- Refuse to accommodate misogynism. Start where you can.

- Reject the label of 'anecdotal evidence.' Embrace your unassailable, personal, lived, and embodied Truths.

- You are exempt from patriarchal assessment. They have no model or monitors capable of evaluating you.

- Remove your attention from the patriarchy. Neither absolve nor vilify them. Give them no power over you.

- Rest securely in your Sovereignty, cherishing your own Divine Design. This is Agency.

Alchemy

Alchemy is not a process; it's a breakthrough, turning a current or longstanding condition into something of a higher order through unanticipated means. Magical realism is a colloidal state, with the rational view of reality combined with or contained within the supernatural. *I'm fairly certain that's my address.*

I recommend we indulge in magical realism until alchemy occurs. We neurodiverse explorers are perfectly outfitted for multi-sensory adventuring. The stretch and reach and holds involved expand our sense of possibility. Like mountain climbers finally reaching a summit and seeing an unimaginably vast ocean on the other side, we need new vistas to inspire us.

As Albert Einstein famously said, "We can't solve our problems by using the same thinking we used when we created them." Alchemy is the creation of something new by inciting change in its basic structure. Try tempting your brain to notice something new with this exercise. Synesthesia is a neurodiverse talent for blending of the senses so that, for example, colors can be heard, smelled, and tasted. This may seem unreasonable until you realize that blueberries do taste blue, and freshly cut grass smells green. *Don't they?*

Our neurodivergent brains operate outside of all sorts of societal norms and built-in filters. Many of us have called a truce with our brains' ingrained devotion to predicting the future based on past experience and their tendency to shield us from new potentials. Alchemy liberates. It is the patriarchy's kryptonite.

We feel truth from our hearts and in our guts and vet it through our own neural networks. The 'ring of truth' is real for us. This is how we create a sanctuary within ourselves, free from patriarchal predators. We become a key in the lock of the patriarchal prisons.

WE are the patriarchy's kryptonite.

Three Little Words

Lynn McIntosh

Check yourself.
And check. Again.
The mirror's cracked; grainy; distorted –
but it'll just have to do, I'm afraid.
So check.
And check. Adjust clothes.
Strike a pose,
And –
Smile. Switched. ON.

You stitched, by hand, a mask
to suit the mood surrounding
but that mood it moved
and rippled
and the threads of that mask
came loose,
no longer fitted.

Quick, stitch it,
before the World looks
too closely.
Before the Moon She spots the ruse
and realises, you don't belong here.
Anywhere. Nowhere.

Tack and fuse
a patchwork cloak,
a shape-shifting cape,
one size fits most.

Over and over
change it to match the nature
of others.

Adjust it here,
re-fit it there.
It pinches for you but as
long as All and Sundry is comfy –
then really
all's well
that mends well.

You snip your ragged edges,
get tangled up in your
threadbare fringe
as you try to keep up with
demands.

Thread, stitch,
still falling apart,
thread, stitch,
at the seams,
thread, stitch,
you can't sew and so...

thread, stitch –
keep unravelling.

Grasping and grabbing.

Grappling
to put all the pieces back and
pull yourself together
but you don't know where all
the bits of you are supposed to go –
never have,
maybe
never will.

You stop.

You can't sew,
you stop.

Disarray. Mess. Chaos
trails.
You're a-frayed.

Ashamed.
Shattered.
Done.

Until at last the Breeze gently shifts and
the cloak slips. Open.
Skin exposed. Bare. But alive.

And the Air She whispers those
three little words...

Autism.
Spectrum.
Disorder.

The Sun joins in the chorus:

You'll be OK.

The Earth now too,
and then sings the Ocean
to the pulse of Her own tides.
Three little words,
always three little words –
You belong here.
We've got you.
Then another voice rumbles.
Subtle. Soft.

A whisper so light
that turns to a roar
and fills up the night:

The Moon.
She sees. Truly sees.
And smiles.

Through silver-streaked tears of
sadness;
joy;
hope;
life.

She sees and says
those three little words.

You are enough.

Rainbow Goddess Guidance

Kay Louise Aldred

Red – Regulate your nervous system
Orange – Open your creative portal
Yellow – Yes! To your truth and full expression
Green – Generate from your genius
Blue – Body comfort priority
Indigo – Initiate from integrity and authenticity
Violet – Vacate the confine of social norms

Radiant Rainbow Ray – celebrate all that you are.

Elk Woman Gentle Born

Lucy Pierce

Conclusion
Trista Hendren

These words did not come to me until Thanksgiving morning—less than a month before we were scheduled to go to print. This was not convenient, given that I had impressed upon my dear circle sister—who tends to run late—in a very Aspie way that she *must* be on time for dinner! Nevertheless, I have realized over the years that my writing comes when it decides to, and not when I will it.

My own neurodiversity has been deeply painful throughout my life.

With that sentence, the tears have come and will probably remain with me for the remainder of this essay.

As a little girl, I was terribly shy and would sit alone on the steps at recess. I went to a small Christian school, and I am still friends with most of my classmates. They were kind and good people—who did try to engage me—and who still indulge my quirkiness—even around the Goddess, which I am sure grates on their nerves.

However, I can still feel the loneliness of those steps. And while I love to be around other people, I still prefer to mostly be alone. I suppose it is familiar—and safe.

I began seeing a psychiatrist when I was 7-years-old. I can still remember the Matisse prints on Dr. Forrester's walls. She was a kind woman, who helped me tremendously—but they still did not know much about neurodiversity in little girls in the early 80's. At 19, she put me on anti-depressants and Ritalin but the Ritalin left me shaky and the Prozac made me feel numb. I did not continue with either prescription. I don't remember her mention ADHD or autism at all, but there is a lot in my life I do not remember.

I still feel at a fundamental level, that something is wrong with me. I have read Kat's poem, *The Neurodivergent Goddess,* in the front of this book dozens, if not hundreds, of times. I still cry through the entire thing. There is something in every piece in this book that deeply resonates with me. I told Kay at one point, that I almost didn't feel like I needed to write a conclusion because *what more could I possibly say?*

As usual, I was bypassing my own healing.

My mother shared that she felt that same recognition and acknowledgment editing this book. But she asked, *what good would a diagnosis do me now that I am approaching my seventies?*

I feel the same nearing 50.

I have identified as *queer* for several decades. I realize that the term is not widely popular anymore but *bi-sexual* does not feel like an adequate description of my sexuality. I have always felt there was something queer—or different—about me. I have identified as an *Aspie* for at least a decade, but that term also seems out of vogue.

I suppose a large part of me does not want to be *anything*. I just want to be *me*. I just want the feeling that something is wrong with me to disappear.

I have watched many friends go through the diagnosis process painfully. My heart is too fragile to do that. We must have a better process. It must be quicker—and it must be more humane. There is NOTHING wrong with any of us. We are just *different*.

Actually, we are not just different. We are *beautiful.* Sometimes our tenderness is overwhelming. Sometimes, our words come out in an autistic, impatient mess that hurt other people. And then we cry—and blame ourselves.

It is time that the world makes some accommodations for the struggles many of us have tried to mask our entire lives.

I have come to a point where I understand my strengths, and I delegate what frustrates me. I know I have tremendous talents, but I am completely helpless in other areas. While I am sure it is unusual for a feminist to be so reliant on her husband, I give Anders tremendous credit for never once putting me down or making me feel unworthy because of my limitations. This is my third marriage. I have had many broken relationships and friendships over the years. Anders is the first person in my life who helped me to recognize my utter wholeness. I don't have to hide with him. This has given me the strength to stop masking with others.

I had an epiphany after chatting with Dr. Stephanie Mines during the last weeks of editing this anthology. Over the last decade, I have focused on the suppression of female wisdom and HERstory. I have sought to bring the Goddess back to the mainstream. But for most of this time, I have been mostly in my head. I am very adept at numbing out and over-working. It is coming back into our bodies that we truly heal. This is no easy task for those of us who are neurodiverse—especially when you add sexual abuse and other trauma into the mix.

The greatest theft to womanity has been being made to feel unworthy and wrong. Those of us who are neurodiverse suffer that shame on a magnified and entirely inhumane level.

We are Divine Rainbow Goddesses. Let us come back to ourselves—and to each other. Let us create a Rainbow Goddess Sisterhood—where we can each find the love and support we crave and deserve.

I hope this book brings comfort to those of us who have suffered in quiet desperation. I dream of a world where people begin to love and accept us as we are. We have much to offer this broken planet.

List of Contributors

Arlene Bailey is a visionary artist and author working in the realm of the Sacred Female in all her many visages. Arlene's paintings and poetry/prose reflect the raw, visceral, and sacred wild in all women, while challenging and questioning everything we know to be true about the who of who we are as women walking in this time.

Through her magical weavings in word and paint—and, drawing on her trainings and skills as an Ordained Priestess, Women's Mysteries Facilitator, Wise Woman Herbalist, Energy Medicine Practitioner and Retired Anthropologist—Arlene invites women to step into personal sovereignty as they listen to their ancient memories and voice of their soul.

Published in several Girl God Books' anthologies, Arlene is also a monthly contributor to *Return to Mago* E-Magazine and has writings in two forthcoming Mago anthologies. Her work can also be found on *The Sacred Wild*, a page on Facebook about re-wilding woman's soul.

This Wise, Wild Crone lives in the Mountains of North Carolina, USA with her cats.

www.facebook.com/sacredwildstudio
www.instagram.com/arlenebaileyartist
www.magobooks.com
www.magoism.net

Arna Baartz is a painter, writer/poet, martial artist, educator, and mother to eight fantastic children. She has been expressing herself creatively for nearly 50 years and finds it to be her favourite way of exploring her inner being enough to evolve positively in an externally-focused world. Arna's artistic and literary expression is her creative perspective of the stories she observes playing out around her. Claims to fame: Arna has been selected for major art prizes and won a number of awards, published many books, and—(her favourite) was being used as a 'paintbrush' at the age of two by well-known Australian artist John Olsen. Arna lives and works from her bush studio in the Northern Rivers, NSW Australia. Her website is www.artofkundalini.com

Barbara O'Meara published writer, co-editor of 'Soul Seers Irish Anthology of Celtic Shamanism', professional visual artist. Exhibitions include 'B.O.R.N. -Babies of Ravaged Nations', group shows Lockhart Gallery New York & 'The Drawing Box' Europe, America, Far East & 'Herstory' Brigid's of the World & Black Lives Matter. Community projects i.e., 'Stitched With Love' Tuam Baby Blanket laid over the burial site at the Mother & Child Home, shown at KOLO International Women's Non Killing Cross Borders Summit in Sarajevo held by Bosnian women survivors. She is continually developing empowering women's 'Art as Activism' events i.e., 'Sort Our Smears' Campaign at 'Festival of FeminismS'. Collections: Microsoft, ESB, Dept Foreign Affairs, Irish Life, Impact Trade Union, Bologna District Council, Behaviour & Attitudes. Art review: "Barbara O'Meara's recent paintings dealing with home and Covid are extremely beautiful and extremely coherent in their communication. Rarely is it seen where painting is used to convey complex emotional human conditions". www.barbaraomearaartist.com

Beth Rees is a purple-haired writer and blogger from Wales (UK). She was diagnosed as autistic with ADHD in December 2021 at the age of 34 after five years of living with a misdiagnosed mental health condition. Beth shares her experiences on her *Just A Square Peg* blog, as well as through upbeat videos on Instagram in the hope of helping other misdiagnosed or late diagnosed women feel they're not alone. She is currently in the middle of writing her first memoir about her misdiagnosis and getting her autism and ADHD diagnosis.

Claire Dorey
Goldsmiths: BA Hons Fine Art.
Main Employment: Journalist and Creative, UK and overseas.

Artist: Most notable group show; *Pillow Talk* at the Tate Modern. Included in the *Pillow Talk Book*.

Curator: 3 x grass roots SLWA exhibitions and educational events on the subject of Female Empowerment, showcasing female artists, academic speeches and local musicians. Silence Is Over – Raising awareness on violence towards women; Ex Voto – Existential Mexican Art Therapy; Heo – Female empowerment in the self-portrait.

Extra study: Suppressed Female History: History of the Goddess; Accessing Creative Wisdom; Sound and Breath Work; Reiki Master; Colour Therapy; Hand Mudras; Reflexology; Sculpture. Teaching Workshops: Sculpture and Drawing.

Deborah A. Meyerriecks lived most of her life in NYC. She is mother to her amazing Dynamic Duo – and she is a dutiful daughter, retired FDNY EMS Lieutenant, practicing witch, community priestess, devoted lover – and is finally learning to be her own best friend. A new author, she has had essays printed in a few Girl God anthologies in the past year before completing and publishing her first book, *Macha and the Medic: Service and Priesthood on the Frontlines of Life*, on her birthday this year. In retirement, she is honored to have been trusted by so many to help guide them into their own shadow journeys to self-understanding. She currently lives in liminal space where the desert and the river and the mountains all meet and share their stories to those who are patient and willing to listen in the Northwest corner of Arizona, USA along the Colorado River. Visit her at www.WillowMoonConsulting.com

Geneviève Labonté has been writing poetry for over 30 years on topics relating to womanhood, spirituality, and recovery from sexual abuse. She shares her poetry via @genevieveswordgarden on Facebook.

Helen Langdon has a degree in English & Art History. She has since seen herself in many guises, beginning with a partial PGCE and followed by stints in the fine art industry, book publishing, fundraising, television programme sales, eleven years as a stay-at-home mum to two girls and now six months as a Teaching Assistant, working 1:1 with children with SEN in a large secondary school. Following her sister's diagnosis with ADHD, she began to suspect the same of herself, which would explain many things! Her poem is based on her experience of supporting a girl at work last term. Helen wrote a lot of poetry in her teenage years, now boxed away in yellowing notepads somewhere in the attic. She has several partial and one complete novel boxed away on her hard drive too.

Holin Kennen is a Southern California native who transplanted herself to Wisconsin in 2004 with her wife and two corgis. She is an ordained Dianic High Priestess who makes magick with the things of the earth: stones, clouds, trees, birds, and plants. Holin spends as much time as she can chopping wood, taking care of her small flock of chickens, gardening, spinning wool and flax, baking bread, and cooking on a wood cookstove. She and her wife live in a Victorian house surrounded by working antiques. She writes a monthly blog – *The Victorian Technology Institute* – describing her adventures in recreating Victorian living.

Jen Wallace is an autistic human (she/her) living on the south coast of Ireland. She is passionate about rewilding, unschooling and deschooling.

She spends her days tending to family, pets, chooks, and the land. She also finds time for writing, arting and working as a Bean Feasa (traditional Irish healer).

Jen and her family have a rewilding project on their land and Jen facilitates foraging and wild medicine walks, women's circles, and workshops in the Work that Reconnects and Nature Resonance. She can be found at: www.instagram.com/jenwallacecreates and https://facebook.com/TheHedgerowProject

Jenny Beech grew up in an army town with four siblings and a forest for company. Despite being a slow reader as a child, she was smitten by a love for stories which spilled over into writing. She writes middlegrade and YA fiction in several genres.

Jenny now lives in Scotland surrounded by bookshops and salt marsh. She is mostly occupied (run ragged) by her two small children and also runs a pottery studio with her partner. It wasn't until her late twenties that Jenny wondered if four neurodivergent close family members, a lifelong habit of perpetual daydreaming and an infamously bad memory might point towards ADHD. She is currently seeking a diagnosis (an ironically difficult task for someone who can't remember appointments) but is wrangling as much humour as she can from the daily fiascos her spicy brain contrives.

Jessica Huff currently works as an analyst for a tech company and in her free time loves to express herself creatively with art and music. She identifies as being neurodivergent having been diagnosed with dyslexia at age 12 and is now pursuing a diagnosis for ADHD in her early 30s. She is a passionate advocate for Diversity, Equity and Inclusion in both her personal and professional life and heads up a focus group on this topic at work.

Jessica Penot is a writer and therapist who lives in Huntsville, Alabama. She specializes in treating trauma and working with adults with autism. She has written 10 books, including the bestseller, *The Accidental Witch*. She is the owner of Tree of Life Behavioral Health.

Kat Shaw prides herself on breaking through the stereotypical views of beauty that have been cast upon society by the media, having made her name painting the glorious reality that is a woman's body.

Her nude studies of real women garnered unprecedented popularity within only a few short months, as women were crying out for themselves to be portrayed in art, rather than the airbrushed images of the perfection of the female form that are so rife in today's culture.

After graduating with a fine art degree, Kat achieved a successful full-time teaching career for 14 years, and continues to teach art part-time whilst passionately pursuing her mission of world domination by empowering as many women as possible to reach their fullest potential by embracing their bodies and loving themselves wholeheartedly.

Kat spreads her inspirational magic through her artwork, her Wellbeing business "Fabulously Imperfect", and her dedication to Goddess energy.

Reiki is a huge part of her life, and as a Reiki Master, Kat is committed to sharing Reiki, teaching Usui, Angelic and Karuna Reiki, and channelling Reiki energy through her artwork to uplift and heal.

As a Sister of Avalon, Kat also works directly with her Goddess consciousness, connecting to Goddess and Priestess energy and translating it into Divine Feminine infused paintings to inspire women and spread Goddess love.

Kat is also mum to a gorgeous teenage daughter, a bellydancer and an avid pioneer to improve the lives of rescue animals.

Kathy Barenskie MSc BSc Ad Dip & Dip. is a Celtic Shamanic Practitioner, Dru Yoga Teacher, and a Meditation Teacher. She also is an accredited Psychodynamic Counsellor, and certified in Shamanic Counselling. She also practices energy healing and is an Usui Reiki Master.

Kathy enjoys writing poetry and creating art from different materials. Kathy lives in the north of Ireland, in a rural town land steeped in history. Being a Sensitive Empath, she practices an Earth magic, and lives by the cycles of the moon.

Katie Bee is a UK-based Writer and Artist with several neurodiverse diagnoses. 'Officially' she has been diagnosed with C-PTSD, Fibromyalgia, Chronic Fatigue Syndrome, and Severe/Recurrent Depressive Disorder. Her own take is that she is recovering from Complex Trauma, is a 'Highly Sensitive Person,' is on the Autistic Spectrum, experiences ADD and SPS, FM and CFS, identifies as all-woman and is a fully paid-up and card-carrying Rainbow Goddess.

Kay Crowder (she/her) lives in a rural area in the state of Colorado in the United States with her 17-yr old daughter, a dog, and two cats. She identifies as neurodivergent and uses writing to process systematic, intergenerational, and childhood trauma. She enjoys reading memoir and historical fiction, spending time in nature, and cultivating community amongst the marginalized.

Kay Louise Aldred (www.kaylouisealdred.com) is a researcher, writer and teacher, who catalyses individual, institutional and collective evolution – through education, embodiment and creativity – amalgamating metacognition, intuition, and instinct.

Her books include: *Mentorship with Goddess: Growing Sacred Womanhood*, published 2022, *Making Love with the Divine: Sacred, Ecstatic and Erotic Experiences* and *Somatic Shamanism: Your Fleshy Knowing as the Tree of Life*, both scheduled for 2023.

Kay and her husband, Dan Aldred, are co-authoring a book together, *Embodied Structure: Creating Safe Space for Learning, Facilitating and Sharing*, scheduled for 2023.

FB, Instagram, Twitter, and LinkedIn @kaylouisealdred

Kerry Purdy is a self-advocate for autism and C-PTSD, as well as a state soldier and search and rescue technician. In her spare time, she enjoys writing, hiking, endurance running, dark yoga, and playing basketball; and she has a shameless stuffed animal collection. She hopes that one day there will be a world where everyone's strengths and talents are acknowledged!

Kim Crowder is a writer, visual artist, and editor. Her writing draws together ethnography, histories, journals, recollections, and reflections. Works exploring relationships between humans, non-humans and the extra-human have been published in various academic essay collections and literary magazines. Her PhD in

Visual Anthropology was awarded by Goldsmiths College, University of London in 2012. Examples of her writing and visuals may be found at http://www.allpicture.co.uk/livesinnature.

Lucy H. Pearce is driven by a need to create, connect and inspire. A best-selling author, vibrant artist, respected publisher and editor, her work focuses on self-knowledge and healing through creativity, archetypes and cyclical living. She gives voice to the soul: the spiritual, the liminal, the darkness and discomfort and the magical in the midst of the mundane. Often described as raw, authentic and life-changing, her work encourages authentic paths to self-expression and is celebrated particularly by highly sensitive and neurodivergent women.

She is drawn to connecting with the seasons of the soul and world through her books, painting, digital art making, clay work, photography and seasonal spirals. She is ever drawn back to the circle and spiral in her ritual and art.

Her award-winning and Amazon best-selling books include: *The Rainbow Way; Burning Woman; Creatrix – she who makes; Moon Time; Medicine Woman* and her most recent, *She of the Sea*. Lucy is the founder and creative director of Womancraft Publishing, established in 2014, which publishes life-changing, paradigm-shifting books by women, for women.

She is the mother of three and lives on the south coast of Ireland.

www.lucyhpearce.com

www.womancraftpublishing.com

Lucy Pierce is living and breathing in the Yarra Valley, Australia, on the unceded lands of the Wurundjeri people, beneath Mt Donna Buang and beside the sibilant Birrarung, with 2 of her 3 beautiful children and a dog called Rue. The last few years have been consumed with running and teaching at a community pottery studio and traversing the underworld to emerge with a qualification as a Soul Centred Psychotherapist. She is looking forward to more space for image making and writing in the coming years, as well as seeking the stillness to be with the beautiful land she calls home. www.lucypierce.com.au

Living in Edinburgh, with her husband and two children, **Lynn McIntosh** is originally from the Isle of Islay. She was diagnosed as Autistic in early 2021, at the age of 36. After attending some support groups she now believes she is also living with ADHD, and it feels like she can finally start truly knowing herself after many years of feeling adrift, and like there was something different about the way she experienced the world, but in a way that she couldn't quite put her finger on or articulate.

So, Lynn is looking on this as the start of her next chapter, maybe even the real starting point of her journey, and she spends her days being as creative as possible in as many different ways as possible. It really is, for her, the best way to interact and communicate with herself and the wider world.

Molly Remer, MSW, D.Min, is a priestess, writer, and teacher facilitating circles and ceremonies in central Missouri. Molly and her husband Mark co-create Story Goddesses at Brigid's Grove (brigidsgrove.etsy.com). Molly is the author of nine books, including *Walking with Persephone, Whole and Holy, Womanrunes,* and the *Goddess Devotional*. She is the creator of the devotional experience #30DaysofGoddess and she loves savoring small magic and everyday enchantment.

Pat Daly (editor) is a mother of three daughters and proud grandma. A published author / writer on career and job search issues, Pat lives in Portland, Oregon.

Schuyler Witman is a queer teacher, healer, parent, witch and undiagnosed adult female autistic person who lives on Salt Spring Island, in British Columbia, Canada.

Dr. Stephanie Mines is the author of five books that reflect over three decades of research as a neuroscientist. She has investigated shock and trauma as a survivor, a professional, a clinical researcher, and healthcare provider. Her nonprofit The TARA Approach is instrumental in the systemic change she promotes as a Regenerative Health paradigm.

Dr. Mines also developed Climate Change & Consciousness to facilitate inner transformation for grounded climate action. Climate Change & Consciousness serves an international and intergenerational community of visionary activists.

In addition, Dr. Mines is an award-winning poet. Her poetry has been published in anthologies and in chapbooks.

Dr. Mines' latest book, *Memoir of An Embryologist: How I Discovered the Secret of Resilience*, will be released in 2023 from Inner Traditions/Sacred Planet Books.

Sylvia Bhagavati is a 55-years-old artist, living in Mexico. She was diagnosed Autistic only a couple years ago. Her work as an artist with Intentional Creativity gears towards mainly autistic girls and women, who so often still go unrecognized. Autism is not Rainman.

She is currently writing her autobiography at: https://www.autobiografiadeunaautista.com

Tamara Albanna is a writer, artist, Reiki Healer, and Tarot reader. After several years of suspecting neurodiversity, she was finally diagnosed with Autism Spectrum in 2021. You can find out more about her and her work at https://tamara-albanna.com.

Trinity Shea Thomas was born neurodiverse. As a child, she was shamed for her gifts. She has spent her life exploring how to move from shrinking from her differences to putting them to work in service.

She is an Irish/Scottish elder storyteller. She weaves stories to catalyze alchemies of pain into meaning, forging paths from apology to superpower.

She is a Prayer Singer. Her vocal sound system creates a container for intention and delivers an infusion of light.

Supports are being created now for Neurodiversity. The best guide was found at the gate of the Oracle of Delphi: "Know Thyself." That's what she does in her Soul Advocacy work. She employs her natural mediumship to help her neurodiverse clients know, refine, and celebrate themselves.

She is a teacher, spiritual counselor, Soul Advocate, and sound shaman. She is Neurodiverse.

She has a home in Colorado, United States, with her husband and two cats.

www.InnerOracle.com

Trista Hendren founded Girl God Books in 2011 to support a necessary unraveling of the patriarchal world view of divinity. Her first book—*The Girl God*, a children's picture book—was a response to her own daughter's inability to see herself reflected in God. Since then, she has published more than 45 books by a dozen women from across the globe with help from her family and friends. She lives in Bergen, Norway. You can learn more about her projects at www.thegirlgod.com.

Wakanda Rose is a Priestess of the Goddess, a Medicine Woman, an Artist and a Musician. She blends Science and Metaphysics together to bring back to life the way of the Goddess in physical reality that is accessible and relatable. She feels a part of her time on Earth is to walk in other's darkness and trauma, reminding people of their worth, guiding them to their own light to re-empower their own selves and being a support to come back to the Goddess way if they so choose. She is an ally to the Plant World with seeing these beings as sacred sentient energy and honours the Herbal Medicine path. Wakanda Rose blends many paths together, honouring each tradition and culture that she gets to experience to re-empower herself and walk the path of the Goddess. You can connect more with Wakanda Rose on Instagram @bywakandarose

Trista's Acknowledgments

I would like to acknowledge my co-editors. My mother, **Pat Daly**, has edited every one of my books. There would be no Girl God Books without her enormous contributions. I was thrilled to also work with **Kay Louise Aldred** and **Tamara Albanna** on this project.

Many thanks to **Lucy H. Pearce** for taking time out of her busy schedule to write the brilliant Preface for this anthology.

Tremendous love and gratitude to **Kat Shaw** for allowing us to feature her gorgeous painting as the cover art.

Enormous appreciation to my husband **Anders Løberg**, who prepared the document for printing and helped with website updates. His love, support and many contributions made this book possible.

I would like to give special acknowledgement to **Dr. Stephanie Mines** for her tremendous therapeutic and written work—which has helped me heal from my childhood sexual abuse—as well as gaining acceptance of myself as I am as a neurodiverse woman.

I would also like to give a shout-out to **Eileen Day McKusick**, whose work with Biofield Tuning has given me so much understanding and compassion of myself and others—and helped me to come back into my body.

Lastly, I would like to thank my dear sisters **Tamara Albanna, Arna Baartz, Susan Morgaine, Desiree Jordan, Jeanette Bjørnsen, Camilla Berge Wolff, Tammy Nedrebø-Skurtveit, Kay Louise Aldred, Sharon Smith, Arlene Bailey, Barbara O'Meara** and **Alyscia Cunningham** for always being right there to cheer me on in the spirit of true sisterhood.

Thank you to all our readers and Girl God supporters over the years. We love and appreciate you!

Kay's Acknowledgments

I'd like to wholeheartedly thank **all the women** who so generously contributed their inspirational stories, visions, poetry, and art to this anthology. Showing up unapologetically and unmasked offers permission to others to do the same – me included.

Gratitude to **Rainbow Goddess** for her gifts and non-conformist glory.

Thank you to **Trista Hendren** for the carnival and celebration Girl God Books is and her tireless trumpeting and showcasing of the creative work of women from all around the globe. Thank you for believing in me – and your yes.

Huge appreciation to Trista's husband, **Anders**, for creating the joyful front cover. Heaps of gratitude also to my other co-editors **Pat Daly** and **Tamara Albanna** and to **Kat Shaw** for the stunning cover art.

And finally – as always – massive love and appreciation for my husband **Dan**, for his support, encouragement and his loving acceptance of our rainbow family and collective divergence.

Tamara's Acknowledgments

To my family who spotted the Autism signs and helped me to embrace them with love and ease. To my team of female therapists who assessed, diagnosed, and walked with me in those first uncertain months. And to the Goddess who loves us all for who we are.

*If you enjoyed this book, please consider writing a
brief review on Amazon and/or Goodreads.*

*We LOVE photos of our readers with Girl God Books! Please post
on social media to spread the word – or email them to
support@girlgod.org.*

What's Next?!

Making Love with the Divine: Sacred, Ecstatic and Erotic Experiences – Kay Louise Aldred

Out of Darkness She Speaks: A Rich Anthology of Poetry and Artwork Inspired by the Feminine – Leonor Murciano-Luna, Ph.D.

Women's Sovereignty and Body Autonomy Beyond Roe v. Wade – Edited by Arlene Bailey, Pat Daly, Sharon Smith, and Trista Hendren

Kali Rising: Sacred Rage – Edited by C. Ara Campbell, Jaclyn Cherie, Pat Daly, and Trista Hendren

Somatic Shamanism: Your Fleshy Knowing as the Tree of Life – Kay Louise Aldred

Embodied Structure: Creating Safe Space for Learning, Facilitating and Sharing – Kay Louise Aldred and Dan Aldred

Pain Perspectives: Finding Meaning in the Fire – Edited by Kay Louise Aldred, Trista Hendren and Pat Daly

Imperfectly Fabulous – Kat Shaw

Anthologies and children's books on the Black Madonna, Mary Magdalene, Mother Mary, Cerridwen, Aradia, Kali, Brigid, Sophia, Spider Woman, Persephone, The Old Antlered One/Ancient Deer Goddess, An' Cailleach and Hecate are also in the works. Details to be announced.

http://thegirlgod.com/publishing.php